Understanding Financial Statements:

A Manager's Guide

Revised Edition

David S. Murphy

Illustrations by Ernest W. Murphy

ISBN-13: 978-1544055091

ISBN-10: 1544055099

Printed and bound in the United States by CreateSpace, an Amazon company.

Understanding Financial Statements:

A Manager's Guide

Contents

	Page
Acknowledgements	vi
Preface	vii
1 Football and Financial Accounting	1
2 What's Mine and What's Not? – The Balance Sheet	19
3 Did I Make Any Money? – The Income Statement	53
4 Where Did the Cash Go? – The Cash Flow Statement	85
5 Putting it all Together – Financial Statement Analysis	101
6 Accounting Choices and Financial Statements	129
Index	173
About the Author	179

Acknowledgements

No book, even one as small as this one, is the work of just one person. It would not have been possible for me to write this had it not been for the patience and understanding of my wife, Heidi Rose, who never seemed to tire of my time in front of the computer. Time in front of the computer also meant time away from my three sons, Geoffrey, Ernest, and Brandon whose support was also invaluable. Ernest redrew the illustrations a number of times, and did so without complaint, so that he could capture the emotion that I wanted to convey.

Several years' worth of MBA students read through this book in manuscript form and patiently endured typos and rewrites. Finally, my colleagues, Dr. Francis Bush and Patrick Mazor read through the final manuscript and their comments greatly improved this small work.

Preface

Financial accounting is history. By that I don't mean that financial accounting is a thing of the past and that it is going the way of the dinosaurs but rather than financial accounting is a specialized and very technical branch of history. Historians may write about events that took place thousands of years ago, or last month. Financial accountants record and report histories of what happened in the recent past, usually the past year. However, the time frame doesn't matter, financial accountants write about history.

As historians, financial accountants face the same philosophical questions that historians in general face every day. Given massive amounts of information about an historical event, what is relevant and will be both interesting and useful to readers of the history? Once the volume of information about an event has been whittled down to a manageable size, how should the information be presented so that it is understandable and relevant? Financial accountants face the same questions every day.

It has often been said that those who don't understand the past are destined to repeat it. We all acknowledge that understanding history is important and that a well-written history can be both engaging and fascinating. History serves important purposes besides entertainment. It explains what happened in the past and why it happened. In addition, once we understand the historical milieu surrounding an event, we can forecast what is likely to occur in the future if we see the same pattern of events and forces coming to play in the present. Financial accounting reports serve that same purposes, they explain what happened in the past, and they can be used to forecast the future. In addition, financial accountants have the same general objectives, to write a history that is both understandable and relevant.

Most historians use words to spin their stories about the past. Financial accountants use numbers. Once you learn how to listen to them, numbers tell stories just as well as do words. You don't need a degree in history to read, understand, and learn from a well-written history. By the same token you don't need a degree in accounting to read and understand financial statements (balance sheet, income statement, statement of changes in stockholders' equity, and cash flow statement). You just need to learn the language that the numbers speak.

The purpose of this book is to provide you with the background and skills that you need as a non-financial manager so that financial statements will talk to you. You will discover that the language that financial statements speak is easy to understand and that the stories that financial statements tell are both fascinating and useful.

David S. Murphy, Ph.D., CPA, CFS
Lynchburg College
Lynchburg, Virginia
15 March 2017

Chapter 1
Football and Financial Accounting

There's no business like show business,
but there are several businesses like
accounting.
David Letterman

The 2011 Discover Orange Bowl was played on January 3, 2011 at the Sun Life Stadium in Miami Gardens, Florida between the Virginia Tech Hokies and the Stanford Cardinals. Stanford defeated Virginia Tech by a score of 40-12. Is that all that you need to know about that game? Is that all that you want to know? For some people that's enough . . . it might even be too much. Other people want to know a little more, others, a lot more. They want answers to some questions.

For example, how did Virginia Tech lose by 28 points when the half-time score was Stanford 13 – Virginia Tech 12? It appeared, at the end of the first half that it was going to be a close game. At the end of the game it seems as if the passing games were close, as were the times of possession and total number of plays. Stanford completed 18 passes for 287 yards to Virginia Tech's 16 completed passes for 224 yards. In addition both teams intercepted one pass. Stanford held the ball for 27 minutes and 46 seconds to Virginia Tech's 32 minutes and 14 seconds of possession. Stanford ran 49 plays to Virginia Tech's 50 plays. So, why the big point differences? To find out what really happened we have to dig a little deeper.

Stanford had a better passing game. While they only average two yards per pass more than Virginia Tech they had a higher completion ratio. Stanford completed 78 percent of its passes while Virginia Tech only completed 48 percent of theirs. But that still doesn't tell the whole story. Stanford carried the ball 31 times to Virginia Tech's 34 carries. If that is all that you know about the ground game then it looks like Virginia Tech had a better game on the ground. Not true. Stanford averaged about 8 yards per carry for a total of 247 yards rushing. Virginia Tech on the other hand averaged about two yards per carry for a total of 67 yards rushing. Stanford gained a total of 534 yards rushing and passing over the course of the game to Virginia Tech's 291 yards.

Now the numbers start to tell a story. It appears that Stanford had a stronger defense. Stanford was able to shut down Virginia Tech's running game, holding them to only 67 yards. Stanford had a stronger offense. They completed a higher percentage of their passes and their ground game bulldozed over Virginia Tech's defense.

Numbers tell stories and well-selected numbers tell good stories. The final score of the Orange Bowl tells what happened; who won and who lost. The game statistics start to answer why and how questions. The same is true in business. Net income (profit or loss) tells how well a company did over the course of a year but it doesn't tell the whole story.

The only ones who can tell the whole story about the 2011 Discover Orange Bowl game were the people who were in the game, the players and the coaches. They can tell you about strategy; what worked and what didn't work. They can tell you about missed blocks and plays where the timing was just a little bit off, or where everything clicked perfectly, like the huge second quarter play by Tyrod Taylor who avoided a sack and then just before going out of bounds threw a touchdown pass to David Wilson. However, for most of us the game statistics provide a pretty complete picture of what happened.

Football is a complex game. The head coach is the Chief Executive Officer. The offensive coach and defensive coach function as chief line officers. The quarterback is charged with strategy implementation, and functions like the Division Manager for the offensive team. The players, in their respective specialties, implement the offensive plan under the quarterback's direction. However, they are not the only ones who make football possible. There are unsung heroes of football who help make the game possible. They are the linesmen, referees, statisticians and score keepers and, for college football, the NCAA.

College football players and their coaches are presumed to know the rules of the game as established by the NCAA. Referees make sure that the rules are followed. The linesmen keep track of the ball placement and out-of-bounds movements. Scorekeepers apply the rules of the game to measure performance . . . to keep score. What would happen to football if there were no rules, no enforcers of the rules, and no score? It would probably turn into uncontrolled mayhem.

Just about everyone likes a good football game. But have you ever thought about what it takes to have a good professional football game? Obviously you need two teams of players. It takes more than that, it takes a lot more. Each team has a head coach and a number of assistant coaches, and they were hired by the owners of the team. Then there is the whole back-office staff . . . the people behind the scenes that you don't see or think about very often unless you place an order for team memorabilia; people like athletic trainers, marketing and promotion specialists, lawyers and accountants, product development specialists and designers . . . and the list could go on.

The teams need a place to play and they also need referees and line judges. The existence of referees and line judges implies a set of rules that everyone agrees to follow. Without rule football would look like disorganized mayhem, wait, that's called rugby isn't it.

Have you ever played a football or basketball game without keeping score? I bet even if you agreed not to keep score; that you kept a mental tally so you would know who won. A football game requires scorekeepers and statisticians as well. Just imagine listening to the sports report on ESPN and hearing a list of the teams that had played on Sunday without any scores. Frustrating.

The captains of industry are the CEO's of major corporations. They have their Chief Financial Officers, Chief Operating Officers, Chief Informational

4

Officers as well and division and line managers. They are the ones that play the game of business. But who sets the rules, and who makes sure that the rules are followed and how is performance measured?

Professional football is a business, and business is like football. Table 1.1 below summarizes the similarities between football and business.

Table 1.1
Football and Business Compared

Football	Business
Team Owners	Stockholders and Board of Directors
Head Coach	Chief Executive Officer
Assistant Coaches	Senior Executive Officers (CFO, COO, etc.)
Players	Line Personnel
Back Office Support	Staff Personnel
NFL	SEC, FASB and IASB
NFL Rules	Generally Accepted Accounting Principles (GAAP), SEC Regulations, IFRS
Scorekeepers and Statisticians	Accountants
Referees and Line Judges	Auditors and Regulators
Playing Field	Economic and Regulatory Environment

Individuals who may not have the time, energy or expertise to create and run a business invest in corporations and become stockholders, the owners. The owners elect a Board of Directors to be their representatives and the Board of Directors in turn appoints the Chief Executive Officer (CEO) to be the "head coach" of the corporation. The CEO selects a group of individuals who will compose the senior executive team. These individuals, just like the offensive or defensive coaches on a football team, are responsible for specific operational activities like finance (Chief Financial Officer), information technology (Chief Information Officer), and operations Chief Operating Officer).

Line personnel are employees involved in the value chain. The value chain is the sequence of events that lead from the development of a product or service, to the provision of that product or service to customers. Back office support personnel, like staff personnel in a corporation, keep the organization running smoothly and support the value-chain activities even though they aren't directly involved in it.

The NFL is the organization that controls professional football and which sets the rules. In the corporate world the Securities and Exchange Commission (SEC) has the legal right under the 1993 and 1934 Securities Acts to set the rules. To a great extent they have let the rule setting function take place in the private sector with the Financial Accounting Standards Board (FASB). FASB, in the United States, is the body that promulgates accounting standards, the rules by which the score is kept. The rules are often referred to as Generally Accepted Accounting Principles or GAAP. The International Accounting Standards Board (IASB) is the authoritative body that sets International Financial Reporting Standards (IFRS) or international GAAP.

Auditors and SEC regulators review the score that has been kept by a corporation and that is reported in corporate financial statements. External auditors issue audit opinions about whether or not the financial statements (the score) are presented in conformity with GAAP (the rules). For that to take place someone has to keep score, and that's where accountants come in.

Not everyone wants to be an NFL scorekeeper or statistician, but I would guess that if you could interview one you would find out that he or she loves the job. The same is true with accountants, not everyone wants to be one, but the game of business would be hard to play if no one kept score.

Accounting

Accounting has been called the language of business. To be successful as a non-financial manager and in business in general you *must* understanding financial statements, the product of the financial accounting process, and the assumptions that underlie those financial statements. The more you understand the score and statistics of a football game, the better you can understand what happened, and the better you can predict what is likely to happen in the next game. Accounting serves the same function.

While there are many definitions of accounting, we are going to define accounting as *the art of recording, classifying and summarizing events and transactions, which are in part at least of a financial nature, and the interpretation thereof.* First of all, accounting is an art, not a science, although some consider it to be a social science. It is a precise art, but there are no natural laws of accounting that theoretical accountants are ever going to discover. As an art, accounting has to be useful. If it ceases to be useful then it will probably disappear.

What!! You want ME to learn accounting?

Progress in football is measured every play by yards gained or lost. In the business world progress is measured by every transaction and that progress is measured in monetary terms. Today computerized accounting systems record, classify and summarize almost all business transactions. Consequently the accountants' key roles are to design and maintain accounting systems, make sure that the computer-based accounting systems are functioning correctly, and to analyze and interpret financial information. Accountants help decision makers understand and use financial information in decision making.

> *Accounting is the art of recording, classifying and summarizing events and transactions, which are in part at least of a financial nature, and the interpretation thereof.*

GAAP

Accounting systems are designed to record, classify and summarize accounting information in conformity with GAAP. So what exactly are GAAP? GAAP, or *generally accepted accounting principles*, are the rules that define how transactions should be recorded and subsequently presented in financial statements.

Following the stock market crash of 1929 Congress passed the 1933 Securities Act. This act specified the accounting and reporting requirements for initial public offerings (IPOs) of securities (stocks and bonds). Congress subsequently passed the 1934 Securities Exchange Act which established the Securities and Exchange Commission (SEC), and also mandated reporting requirements for securities traded in the secondary market, the stock exchanges. The 1934 Act also gave the SEC the right and responsibility to set accounting and reporting standards for companies whose securities are publically traded. For the most part the SEC has delegated the standard setting process to the private sector. Today the Financial Accounting Standards Board, FASB, sets accounting standards for for-profit and private, not-for-profit entities in the United States.

U.S. GAAP is not used around the world. In fact, in most countries the Ministry of Finance is charged with the responsibility of setting accounting standards. In many countries those standards are based on International Financial Reporting Standards (IFRS). IFRS are promulgated by the International Accounting Standards Board (IASB). The SEC announced its plan for convergence with IFRS in 2008.

The SEC published a statement of continued support for a single set of high-quality global accounting standards in February of 2010 and acknowledged that IFRS is best positioned to serve in that role. The SEC staff provided an update regarding progress towards completing the IFRS work plan at the December 2011 AICPA annual conference. The SEC staff indicated they would need additional time to complete a final report on the work plan and to make a recommendation to the Commission on whether, when, and how to further incorporate IFRS into the U.S. financial reporting system. Finally in 2014 the SEC backed away from the plan to implement IFRS and it now looks like U.S. companies will continue to prepare their financial statements in conformity with GAAP.

Figure 1.1 below identifies the key players in the accounting standards setting process. The FASB Statements of Financial Accounting Concepts provide the theoretical framework that we will use to understand financial statements and the effects of accounting choices on those statements.

The structure and concepts of these Concept Statements are summarized in Figure 2. The remainder of this chapter will focus on the objectives, qualitative characteristics, constraints and transaction recognition and measurement concepts that affect financial statements. We will delve into the financial statements in subsequent chapters.

Financial Reporting Objectives

The overriding objective of financial reporting is to provide decision useful information to the users of financial statements. The accounting profession makes the assumption that the core financial statements listed in Figure 1.2 in the basic financial statement block are relevant to all decision makers, regardless of the kind of financial decision that they make. This means that a balance sheet, income statement, and statement of cash flows are deemed to be relevant to creditors, potential creditors, investors, potential investors, regulators, suppliers, customers, employees and anyone else who has to make a financial decision about the company.

The second objective of financial reporting is to provide information that can be used to predict cash flows. Net income is presumed to be a good predictor of future net income. However, it is not a good predictor of future cash flow. It took a long time for the accounting profession to recognize that a company can't pay its bills with net income. It needs cash. The statement of changes in financial position, evolved from the early 1970's to become the statement of cash flows in 1987 that we use today.

Figure 1.1
Key Standards Setting Players

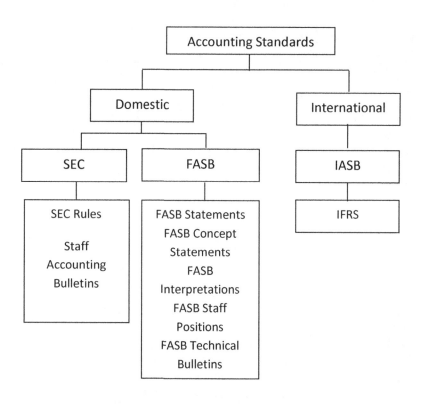

Figure 1.2
FASB Financial Accounting Concepts

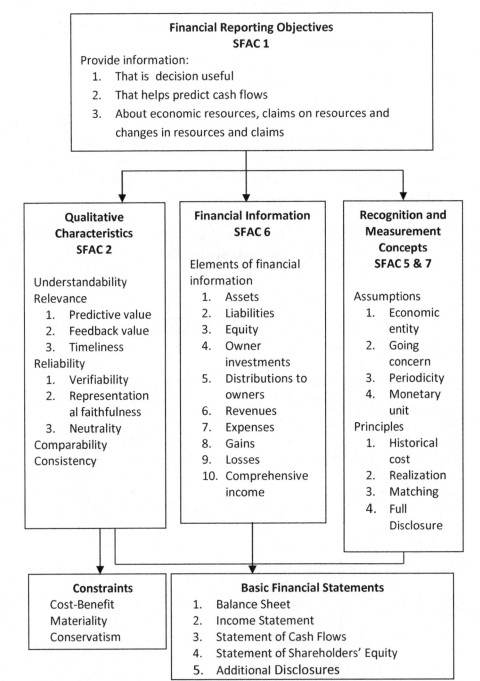

The final financial reporting objective is that financial information should provide information about resources that an organization owns or controls, and claims against those resources.

Qualitative Characteristics of Financial Information

SFAC 2 defines the qualitative attributes that make financial accounting information useful. We will return to these characteristics from time to time throughout this book to understand why accountants do what they do. The first qualitative characteristic is understandability.

Understandability – The overarching qualitative characteristic of financial information is that it should be understandable. Information, no matter how precise or voluminous, is of no value if the user of the information can't understand it. Unfortunately financial information is not always easy to understand, and unless an individual understands the assumptions behind the information it can even be misleading.

Constraints – Information presented in financial statements is subject to three constraints: the cost-benefit tradeoff, materiality, and conservatism. The cost-benefit constraint asserts that information should not be provided if the cost of acquiring and presenting the information is greater than its decision value. For example, I doubt that you would hire a $200 per hour consultant for a day to make a $1,000 decision. It just wouldn't be worth it.

Materiality – The materiality constraint directs that information that is not material need not be presented. Information is material if its knowledge would make a difference to a decision maker. We all have different materiality thresholds, points where something makes a difference to us or it doesn't. We also apply different personal materiality criteria in different situations. For example, assume that you are waking down the street and see a penny. Will you stop and pick it up or will you keep on walking? Most people that will step on the penny and keep on walking. But what if the coin was a quarter? Now would you stop and pick it up? Again, most people that I know will bend over, pick the quarter up and put it in their pocket. Somewhere between a penny and a quarter they have a materiality threshold.

Now assume that you are driving home and see the glint of a shiny quarter on the curb. Will you park your car, get out, and retrieve the quarter? Probably not. On the other hand, what if you have great eyes and spy a $100 bill on the curb. Now will you stop? Probably. A quarter was material when walking but not when you were driving. You just demonstrated different materiality thresholds in different situations.

This same concept applies to financial statements as well. Walmart's 2011 annual report showed net sales of $418,952 and a little note at the top of the page indicated that all amounts were in millions so their net sales were really about $418,952,000,000. Walmart management and its auditor decided that anything less than $1,000,000 was not material so they rounded amounts to the nearest million. As you analyze financial statements remember that someone established a materiality threshold.

Conservatism – The final constraint is conservatism. Conservatism states that accountants and auditors, if they make a mistake, will try to err on the side of conservatism; the side where they would do the least harm. Figure 3 below shows possible financial statement outcomes and condition states.

Figure 1.3
Financial Statement Outcomes

Reported Condition of the Financial Statement	*Actual Condition of the Financial Statement*	
	Fairly Presented	*Not Fairly Presented*
Fairly Presented	Correct Decision	Type I Error
Not Fairly Presented	Type II Error	Correct Decision

As Figure 1.3 illustrates, when a financial statement really is fairly presented and the auditor and management report that it is so, the right decision has been made. The same is true when a financial statement is not fairly presented and auditors and management so state. In the Error I cell the financial statement is not fairly presented, it misstates financial reality and may even be fraudulent. However, auditors failed to recognize the misstatement and reported that the financial statements were fairly presented. Users of the financial statements are likely to rely on the auditor's assertion to their detriment.

In the Error II cell auditor and management assert that financial information is not fairly presented when in reality it is. This may cause users of the financial information to expend additional time and resources to gather and analyze more information before they make a decision. However, their ultimate decision is less likely to cause them significant financial harm. Accountants and auditors, because of the principal of conservatism, make decisions that increase the likelihood that they make Type II errors rather than Type I errors. For this reasons accountants may be slow to recognize revenue but accelerate the recognition of expenses. They would rather understate net income than overstate it.

Relevance – The two most important qualitative characteristics of accounting information are relevance and reliability. Information is considered to be relevant if it can be used to predict the future (predictive value) or to explain the past (feedback value). In addition, to be relevant, information must be timely. That means that decision makers receive the information in time to incorporate it into their decision process.

Reliability – Information is considered to be reliable if it is verifiable, is representationally faithful, and if it is unbiased or neutral. You never know in business if the decision that you made was the best decision or the "right" decision and the same is true in accounting and auditing. Accountants have replaced the concept of "rightness" with verifiability. This means that two accountants, given the same experience and the same set of facts, would come to the same conclusion.

Representational faithfulness asserts that information represents what we say that it does. As you will see in the chapter on the Balance Sheet the assumption of representational faithfulness is one of the current difficulties in accounting.

Whoever controls information can control how decisions are made. If someone provides you with incomplete information, for example only good information about one alternative and incomplete and negative information about another alternative, and you trust the individual who provided the information that person is able to influence the alternative that you select. Accountants realize that if they try to lead decision processes by selectively providing information that they will lose credibility and will no longer be trusted sources of information and financial advice. Consequently accountants and auditors jealously guard their position of neutrality.

Consistency and Comparability – To analyze trends and changes over time it is necessary to compare financial statements over time, for example to compare this year's income statement with last year's. In addition, it is often useful to compare the financial statements of different companies. Consistency and comparability work together to facilitate within company comparisons over time, and between company comparisons at a point in time.

The consistency principle asserts that a company should use the same accounting principles, the same GAAP, from one period to another. This provides for intra-firm consistency of financial statements over time. The comparability principle asserts that different companies in the same industry should use the same GAAP at the same point in time. This provides for inter-firm comparability at a point in time.

Transaction Recognition and Measurement Concepts

Assumptions that underlie accounting include the entity concept, the going concern principle, periodicity, and the stable monetary unit assumption. Principles that have led to the development of GAAP include the historical cost principle, the revenue recognition or realization principle, the matching principle and full disclosure.

Entity Concept – The entity concept provides the basis for treating an organization or a part of an organization as a distinct entity for accounting purposes. For example, assume that you own a business as a sole proprietor.

While you and the business are the same legal entity, you can be considered to be separate accounting entities and personal and business financial statements could be prepared. By the same token, although a corporation is one legal entity it is possible to identify different sub-entities, for example divisions, and prepare both corporate and divisional financial statements.

Going Concern – The going-concern assumption states that a business will be treated as if it will continue for the foreseeable future as a going concern unless there is evidence to the contrary. Accounting rules change dramatically when a business is no longer considered to be a going concern. Auditors in particular, are very cautious about stating that a business is no longer a going concern because they don't want to make a self-fulfilling prophecy and cause an otherwise viable company to fail.

Periodicity – The Time-Period Concept – Corporations can have extremely long lives. For example, Beretta, the Italian gun manufacturer, was founded in 1526. Beretta management can't wait until the company folds to find out if it made a profit. The time-period concept states that accounting takes place over discreet periods of time and that financial statements can be prepared for each of those time periods. Time periods should be equal in length and provide for timely reporting of information. Corporations prepare quarterly and annual financial reports because of the periodicity concept.

Stable-Monetary-Unit Assumption – Accountants assume that the value of the monetary unit they are using, whether it is the dollar or a foreign currency, will remain stable over time. This allows accountants to record transactions without having to worry that one dollar today doesn't have the same purchasing power as one dollar that was spent years ago. Accountants realize that inflation does occur, but they do not adjust the accounting records for inflation. FASB Statement 33, titled "Financial Reporting and Changing Prices", was issued in 1979 when the inflation rate in the United States reached historically high level. This statement required the measurement and disclosure of information on the effect of changing prices on the financial statements. The implementation of FASB 33 was made voluntary by FASB 89 in 1986, which was then amended by FASB 139 in 2000. The result, because inflation rates are now at historically low levels, is that most companies assume a stable monetary unit and they do not report price change information.

Historical Cost Principle – The historical cost principle states that the actual cost of an item (asset or service) should be used to record the item in the accounting records. This principle is made possible in part by the stable monetary unit assumption and also by the principles of verifiability and neutrality. The acquisition cost of an item is both verifiable (any one can look at the purchase documents) and neutral (unlike an appraised value). While the historical cost principle applies to most items a few items, for which there is an open market with verifiable prices, are valued at current market value.

Revenue (Realization) Principle – The revenue principle states that revenue should be recorded when it is earned and not before. Accountants usually recognize revenue when it has been earned, when the amount earned can be determined, and when it is reasonably probable that the customer will pay the amount owed.

Matching Principle – The matching principle states that an organization should make every effort to match expenses with the revenues earned during the period. The three most common approaches to matching are (1) cause and effect, (2) systematic and rational allocation, and (3) immediate recognition. Under cause and effect matching expenses, like a sales commission, are tied to the revenue that the expense-causing activity generated. When an expenditure, for example the purchase of a piece of assembly line equipment, is likely to be used over a number of accounting periods its cost is allocated systematically and rationally to the accounting periods that benefit from the use of the equipment. Finally, if an expenditure cannot be matched to a revenue generating activity and it doesn't provide future economic benefits then it is immediately recognized as an expense.

Full-Disclosure Principle – The full-disclosure principle states that an organization's financial statements should contain all relevant data about the operations and financial position of the organization. In other words, the reports should provide enough information that outsiders can make knowledgeable decisions about the organization. An organization should report the accounting methods that it is using since these methods may affect the way that profit or loss is measured and the valuation of the organization's economic resources. In addition the accountings methods used affect how an outsider would compare one organization to another. The full-disclosure principle requires that footnotes and supporting schedules be prepared to explain the nuances of the information provided in the basic financial statements.

Conclusion

In this chapter I have tried to set the stage for accounting by comparing it to football. I hope that you see that accountants, like scorekeepers and statisticians, provide useful information about how the game of business is being played and who the winners that the losers are. Auditors play the role of the referees in a football game, ensuring that rules (GAAP) are consistently followed.

In the second half of the chapter I provided you with an overview of accounting theory. We will come back to the theory concepts like historical costs and revenue recognition in the following chapters as we examine the primary financial statements and the effects of accounting choices on the financial statements.

18

Chapter 2
What's Mine and What's Not – The Balance Sheet

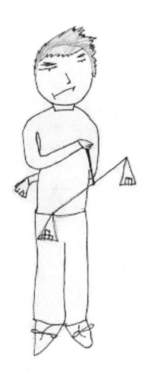

Is this right? Shouldn't this balance?

The balance sheet is the oldest of the primary financial statements. It originated centuries ago with international trading ventures in Italy. An entrepreneur would seek funding for a business trip to the Orient and form a business venture. Once the trip was successfully concluded and the merchandise had been sold the remaining balances were divided between the entrepreneur and the investors.   The balance sheet evolved to provide a picture, a snap shot, of a firm's financial position at a point in time.

The Accounting Equation

The balance sheet balances; hence its name. It shows the equality of the accounting equation:

$$Assets = Liabilities + Owners'Equity$$

Assets are the economic resources owned or controlled by a business. Assets include things like cash, accounts receivable, inventory, equipment, vehicles and buildings. Assets also include legal rights that have economic value, things like copyrights and trademarks.   Assets are usually divided into at least three different categories:

- Current assets,
- Property, plant and equipment, and
- Intangible assets.

Current assets, in general, are assets that will be used or converted into cash within a year. Property, plant and equipment are assets that have a long life and will be used over a number of years. Intangible assets are economic resources, like patents and trademarks, that don't have a physical substance but which have economic value.

One of the following accounts is *not* an asset. Which one is it?

- Cash
- Accounts receivable
- Inventory
- Accounts payable
- Office equipment

Check the box below for the answer . . . but give it a try first.

Liabilities are the obligations that a business has to pay. Current liabilities are debts that will be paid within a year while long-term debts, like a 30-year mortgage, will be paid over a longer period of time. The payment of liabilities usually requires the expenditure of a current asset, like cash, or the creation of another current liability. You have probably heard of people who will pay off a credit card balance by opening another credit card and transferring the balance from the first credit card to the second, ostensibly because the second credit card had a lower initial interest rate. They really didn't reduce their liabilities; they just traded one current liability for another.

> Accounts payable are not assets, they are liabilities.

Owners' equity represents the residual claim that the owners have on the assets of a business after all of the liabilities have been paid. Remember that the accounting equation states that assets are equal to liabilities plus owners' equity. We can rearrange the terms in the accounting equation and rewrite it as:

$$Assets - Liabilities = Net\ Assets = Owners'Equity$$

and

$$Net\ Assets = Owners'Equity = Net\ Worth$$

The most common forms of owners' equity are the investments that the owners of the corporation make in the stock of the company, or the equity investments of partners in a partnership. When a business earns a profit it has *net income*. The net income that is not distributed to stockholders as dividends stays in the firm and is used by management to grow the company. This undistributed net income is recorded as *retained earnings* in the owners' equity part of a balance sheet.

Balance Sheet

Let's take a look at a simple balance sheet. As noted above, the accounting equation shows that assets are equal to the sum of liabilities and owners' equity. The balance sheet shows this equality. Figure 2.1 shows that a balance sheet must balance.

Figure 2.1

The Accounting Balance

Assets   Liabilities +
                          Owners' Equity

It is often said that good accountants never lose their balance. This is because the accounting equation and thus the balance sheet must always balance. Obviously if we add weight to the left hand side of the balance scale above we will have to add the same weight to the right hand side or the balance will be out of balance. Alternatively, we could also substitute one equal weight for another on the left-hand side of the scale and it would still balance. For example if a company uses cash to purchase inventory it has substituted or exchanged one asset (inventory) on the left-hand side for another asset (cash).

Assume that a business person started a new business by incorporating it as Kids' Klothes, and then investing $10,000 in the corporation in exchange for common stock. The owner then went to the bank and borrowed another $20,000 on a short-term loan and purchased the following:

- Store furniture and fixtures $ 8,000
- Inventory $10,000

Thus the business exchanged $18,000 of the cash that it had for other assets, leaving cash of $12,000. The balance sheet prepared on June 30, 2013, the day before the grand opening the business, Kids' Klothes, is shown in Figure 2.2 below.

The first thing to notice about the balance sheet is that it is dated as of a specific date. The balance sheet is a snap shot, a picture, at a specific point in time. If Kids' Klothes prepared a balance sheet on July 1, 2013, the very next day of business, it would look different from the one that you see below because business events would have changed the balances of the accounts. Also note that the balance sheet balances. Total assets are equal to total liabilities plus owners' equity, and that means that the accounting equation for Kids' Klothes is in balance. But, what else does it tell you?

Figure 2.2
Kids' Klothes
Balance Sheet
June 30, 2013

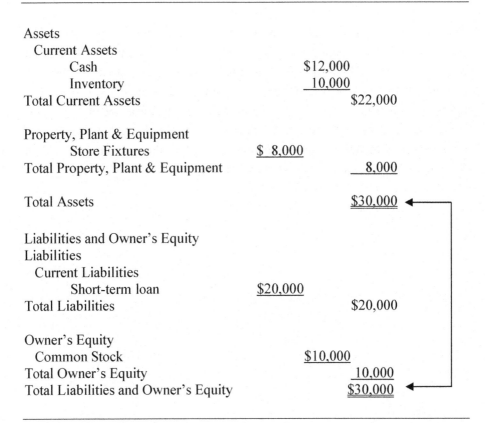

Assets			
Current Assets			
Cash		$12,000	
Inventory		10,000	
Total Current Assets			$22,000
Property, Plant & Equipment			
Store Fixtures	$ 8,000		
Total Property, Plant & Equipment			8,000
Total Assets			$30,000
Liabilities and Owner's Equity			
Liabilities			
Current Liabilities			
Short-term loan	$20,000		
Total Liabilities			$20,000
Owner's Equity			
Common Stock		$10,000	
Total Owner's Equity			10,000
Total Liabilities and Owner's Equity			$30,000

Accountants will tell you that the balance sheet shows a company's financial position. That may not be too helpful if you don't know what they mean by "financial position". All financial position really means was shown in the equation:

$$Assets - Liablilites = Net\ Assets = Owners'Equity = Net\ Worth$$

The balance sheet shows us the historical cost (for the most part) of the assets that the business owns or controls, its liabilities, and its net worth. The balance sheet, however, doesn't tell us what the company is worth.

Let's take a quick look at Kids' Klothes through the lens of the accounting equation. Remember that

$$Assets = Liabilities + Owners'Equity.$$

Does that equation hold for Kids' Klothes? Let's pull some numbers down from the balance sheet and see. From Kids' Klothes balance sheet we know that:

- Total Assets = $30,000,
- Total Liabilities = $20,000, and
- Total Owners' Equity = $10,000.

When we plug those numbers into the accounting equation we get the following:

$$Assets = Liabilities + Owners'Equity$$

$$\$30,000 = \$20,000 + \$10,000$$

We can also check the net asset or net worth form of the accounting equation.

$$Assets - Liablilites = Owners'Equity = Net\ Assets = Net\ Worth$$

$$\$30,000 - \$20,000 = \$10,000$$

We now know that owners' equity, which is equal to net assets or net worth, is $10,000.

Market Cap

The best measure of what a company is worth is what someone would pay for it. We can estimate that amount by looking at a company's market capitalization (market cap). Market cap is the product of the number of shares of stock that a company has sold times its current market price.

Market Capitalization
= Number of Share Outstanding x Market Price per Share

On January 14, 2012, Walmart Stores, Inc. had a market cap of $228,910,000,000 however its balance sheet, in Figure 2.3 below, showed the following.

Figure 2.3
Walmart Stores, Inc.
Summary Balance Sheet
January 30, 2012

Total assets	$193,406,000,000
Total liabilities	$121,687,000,000
Total Stockholders' Equity	71,315,000,000
Total Liabilities & Equity	$193,406,000,000

This means that there was a $157,595,000,000 difference between Walmart's market cap, what the stock market thought that the company was worth and its net worth on the balance sheet ($157,595,000 = $228,910,000,000 - $71,315,000,000).

What Went Wrong?

What went wrong with the balance sheet? Why doesn't it show what a company is worth? There are a couple of answers to this representational faithfulness question. First of all, Walmart Stores, Inc., like most companies has invested in developing human resources. The management skills, knowledge and experience of employees are assets. They have value. Unfortunately the value of those human assets is hard to measure and so it is not included on the balance sheet. Many other assets, like a company's name recognition, loyal customer base, and image also have real economic value but are hard to measure. In addition market cap takes into account the future earning potential of the company. The bottom line is that a lot of real economic resources and values that the stock market recognizes and imputes into stock prices are not measured by accountants and consequently are excluded from balance sheets.

Most assets on the balance sheet are recorded and reported at historical cost. Recall that historical cost was the price paid when an asset was purchased. Some assets decrease in value over time, others may increase. Most increases in value are not recognized on the balance sheet until the company sells the asset. For example, and this is a real case, assume that a wise investor purchased a square block of downtown Seattle in the 1930's for about $50,000. Today that land is owned by a trust that was established by the investor. Major corporations have leased the land from the trust and, at the end of the lease the land and all improvements upon it (the buildings) revert to the trust. How would you value the land on that trust's balance sheet?

The right answer is $50,000 because that is the historical acquisition cost of the land. However, the land might be worth $2 billion today. Nevertheless, presenting the land at its current value would violate GAAP. The historical cost principle requires that all non-monetary assets be reported at cost, not market value. This principle is the other factor that results in the balance sheet's representational faithfulness problem.

Most people think that a balance sheet shows what a company is worth. It doesn't. It shows the aggregate historical cost of acquired assets and the creditor and owner claims against those assets. So what good is a balance sheet?

Why Use a Balance Sheet?

One of the most important uses of the balance sheet today is to assess a company's ability to meet its debt obligations. This is called liquidity analysis. The balance sheet can also be used to perform a form of risk assessment on a company. We do this by looking how a company has funded its operations; the relationship between debt and equity. This is referred to as leverage analysis. Balance sheets, in combination with the income statement, can also be used to determine how well a company is managing its assets, and generating and using cash. We will look at asset management and profitability assessment issues in the next chapter.

Liquidity Analysis – Three common measures of a company's ability to meet it short-term debt obligations are (1) working capital, (2) current ratio, and (3) acid-test ratio. Current liabilities are paid with current assets, usually cash. Working capital is:

$$Working\ Capital = Current\ Assets - Current\ Liabilities$$

Positive working capital means that a company has more current assets than current liabilities and so, given enough time, should be able to meet its current debt obligations. As of January 31, 2012 Walmart Store, Inc. had current assets of about $55 billion dollars and current liabilities of $62 billion dollars. This means that they had negative working capital of $7 billion. That means that Walmart, on January 31, 2012, didn't have sufficient current assets to cover its current debt obligations.

The current ratio is the second common measure of liquidity. It is computed as:

$$Current\ Ratio = \frac{Current\ Assets}{Current\ Liabilities}$$

Walmart's current ratio, using the 2012 amounts was (all amounts are in billions of dollars):

$$Current\ Ratio = \frac{\$55}{\$62} = 0.89$$

A good rule of thumb is that the current ratio should be about 2:1 or 2.0. This means that in general a company should have twice as much in current assets as it does in current liabilities.

Current assets include a number of items that can't be converted into cash quickly. For example, customer receivables (the money that customers owe the business) has to be collected before it can be used to pay debts. Inventory has to be sold and then any resulting receivables have to be collected. The acid-test ratio or quick ratio provides a good measure of whether or not a company could meet its current debt obligations *today* if it had to. It is calculated as:

$$Acid - Test\ Ratio$$
$$= \frac{Cash + Accounts\ Receivable + Short\ term\ investments}{Current\ Liabilites}$$

Walmart's acid-test ratio was (all amounts are in billions of dollars):

$$Acid - test\ Ratio = \frac{\$14.3}{\$62.0} = 0.23$$

A common rule-of-thumb for the acid-test ratio is that it should be at least 1:1 or 1.0. Thus it would appear that Walmart in 2012 had a liquidity or cash-flow problem which translates into business risk.

A one-period analysis of financial ratios can be useful. However, you will learn more if you look at trends over time and/or compare ratios for similar businesses. For example, you might want to compare Walmart and Target financial ratios as shown in Figure 2.4.

Figure 2.4
Walmart and Target
Liquidity Ratio Comparison
January 30, 2012

Liquidity Measure	Walmart	Target
Working Capital	$-7.3 billion	$2.2 billion
Current Ratio	0.89	1.50
Acid-test Ratio	0.23	0.78

If you were a banker, which company would you rather loan money to? Which company, just based on this analysis, has a higher default risk? Which company appears better able to pay its current obligations?

Leverage Analysis – Leverage is a way of using other people's money to make your money work harder. In business that means using debt to help finance operations rather than relying exclusively on stockholder investments and the cash generated by the business. We will look at how leverage can affect profitability measures in a later chapter. Right now let's look at the cash-flow advantage provided by leverage, then will look at one measure of leverage.

Leverage is a measure of how much debt a company uses to finance its operations.

Assume that a company needs to raise additional capital to fund a new project, and that it pays a 40 percent tax rate. One alternative is to sell bonds, a form of debt, and then pay interest on the bonds until they mature and have to be repaid. The other option is to sell stock to raise the needed capital. Of course the stockholders will expect a return on their investment so they will clamor for dividends. To make the analysis simple, further assume that if the company sell bonds it will pay $1,000,000 per year in interest. On the other hand, if it issues new shares of stock, it will have to pay out an additional $1,000,000 in dividends. Moreover, some day the bonds will have to be repaid. Stockholder investments, unless a corporation is liquidating, are permanent investments that do not have to be repaid.

Interest payments are tax-deductible expenses, dividends are not. Because interest expense on the bonds will reduce taxable income, the interest will also reduce the company's tax bill. Dividends, unfortunately for the company, are not tax deductible so their payment doesn't affect corporate taxes. The after-tax cash-outflow from the interest payment will be $600,000, ($1,000,000 x (1-.40)). The after-tax cash-outflow from paying dividends will be $1,000,000. Thus paying interest on the bonds requires less cash than does paying dividends.

The down side of debt is that it has to be repaid. As long as a company is generating sufficient funds to meet periodic interest payments and to make the eventual principle repayment that isn't too much of a problem. However, if a company falls on hard times, or the economy experiences a down turn, it may not be able to make those required payments. Debt increases risk for a company because it increases the possibility of bankruptcy. One of the key issues in financial management is to select the optimal debt level, a level that will improve profitability and cash flow without substantially increasing default risk.

The most common measure of leverage is the debt-to-equity ratio, or simply the debt ratio. It is computed as:

$$Debt\ Ratio = \frac{Total\ Debt}{Total\ Equity}$$

The debt, equity and debt ratios for Walmart and Target are compared in Figure 2.5 below. Both Walmart and Target are highly leveraged.

Walmart has 1.70 times as much debt as equity. Target has 1.95 times as much debt as equity, or 195 percent more debt than equity. Sears, on the same date, had a debt ratio of 3.99 (total debt of $17.1 billion divided by total equity of $4.281 billion). They have 399 percent more debt than equity.

Which of the three retailers do you think has the highest level of default risk? If you were a banker which company do you think you might steer clear of?

Figure 2.5
Walmart and Target
Debt to Equity Comparison
January 30, 2012

Leverage Measure	Walmart	Target
Total Debt	$121.7 billion	$30.8 billion
Total Equity	$ 71.7 billion	$15.8 billion
Debt Ratio	1.70	1.95

Another Look

The Kids' Klothes balance sheet that we have looked at in this chapter was pretty simple. We should take a look at a more complex, classified balance sheet so that you get use to reading and analyzing complex balance sheets.

A classified balance sheet shows sub-categories within the assets, liability and owners' equity sections. The asset section is usually divided into current asset; property, plant and equipment (long-lived assets); intangible asset, and other asset sections. As a convention, current assets are usually listed in decreasing order of liquidity. Liquidity, as used here, is a measure of the ease and speed with which an asset can be converted to cash. Obviously then cash would appear first.

The liability section is subdivided into current liability and long-term liability sections. A current liability is usually defined as an obligation with will be paid within one year, or that will require the expenditure of a current asset. Long-term liabilities are obligations that will be paid more than one year in the future. For example, if a company sold a 10-year bond, a bond that would be repaid ten years in the future, the bond would be classified as a long-term liability. The portion of a long-term liability that must be paid within one year of the balance sheet date should be classified as a current liability.

The owners' equity section of a classified balance sheet usually does not have subsections. It does, however, have a number of interesting accounts. Two of the most common accounts are common stock and retained earnings. The common stock account shows the amount that owners have invested in the company by purchasing common stock from the company (the value of stock purchased on a stock exchange from other stockholders is not shown on the balance sheet). The balance sheet usually shows the *par value* of the stock that has been purchased by stockholders.

Par value is the legal capital of a corporation. Par value is established in the articles of incorporation when a corporation is formed and the par value or legal capital amount cannot be distributed to stockholders unless the corporation is liquidating. Par value is usually set at a very low dollar amount, for example $1.00, which gives corporate management more flexibility.

This also means that if stockholders purchase stock from the corporation for a price that is greater than the par value of the stock then the excess of the selling price of the stock over par value must be recorded in another account. For example assume that a corporation sold 1,000 shares of $1.00 par value common stock to a stockholder for $5.00 per share to form a new corporation. The excess of the sales price of the stock is $4.00 (selling price – par value). The stockholder equity section of the balance sheet would report the following:

Common stock, $1.00 par, 1,000 shares $1,000

Paid-in Capital in Excess of Par $4,000

The new account, paid-in capital in excess of par, is where the difference between the selling price of stock and its par value is recorded.

Oftentimes you will see three other numbers in the description of common stock on the balance sheet. These numbers are "authorized", "issued" and "outstanding". The number of shares authorized is the total number of shares, according to the articles of incorporation, which a corporation is allowed to sell. The number of share issued is the number of shares that have ever been sold to stockholders. The number of shares outstanding is the number of shares *currently* owned by external stockholders.

You might wonder why there would ever be a difference between the number of shares issued and outstanding. Sometimes a corporation will purchase its own stock on the open market. That stock, purchased from stockholders by the corporation, can be retired. Retired stock is no longer considered issued or outstanding. Alternatively the shares can be held for resale. These shares of stock are called *treasury stock* and reduce the number of shares outstanding but not the number of shares issued. Corporations purchase treasury stock for a number of reasons. One common reason is to have shares of stock available to fund employee stock option compensation plans.

Let's assume the following set of facts in another example:

1. A corporation is authorized to sell 100,000 shares of $1.00 par common stock.
2. It has sold 20,000 shares of common stock for an average price of $8.00 per share.
3. This year the corporation purchased 1,000 shares of treasury stock for $9.00 per share.

What would you expect to see in the owners' equity section of the balance sheet? Give it some thought and then look in the box on the next page.

Common Stock, $1.00 par, 100,000 shares authorized, 20,000 share issued, 19,000 shares outstanding	$ 20,000
Paid-in Capital in Excess of Par	$140,000
Treasury Stock	($ 9,000)
Total Owners' Equity	$151,000

Note: Accountants use brackets to identify negative numbers and to imply subtraction as in the ($ 9,000) above.

Well, how did you do? The common stock account shows the par value of the shares issued, not the shares outstanding. The paid-in capital in excess of par account shows the difference between the average selling price and the par value of the shares issued. The treasury stock account has a negative balance, and shows the purchase price of the 1,000 shares that the company bought on the open stock market. When we subtract the treasury stock balance from the total of common stock and paid-in capital in excess of par we get the value of the common stock outstanding.

Sometimes a corporation will have more than one class of stock. The most common second class of stock is preferred stock. Table 2.6 below summarizes the differences between common stock and preferred stock. As you will note in the table, there are some significant differences between preferred and common stock.

Table 2.6
Common and Preferred Stock Attributes

Attribute	Common Stock	Preferred Stock
Participation in management	Right to vote at the annual meeting of the stockholders	No voting rights

Attribute	Common Stock	Preferred Stock
Right to maintain ownership percentage (the preemptive right) when additional shares of stock are offered for sale by the corporation.	Yes, this is a right of first refusal.	No
Order of claims on residual assets at liquidation	After preferred stockholders	Before common stockholders
Order of claims on dividends	After preferred stockholders	Before common stockholders
Dividend amount	Set by board of directors	Stated as a percentage of par or stated value in the articles of incorporation
Right to prior year dividend amount if no dividends were paid in the prior year (dividends in arrears)	No right	Right may exist. It is called the *cumulative* right. If the cumulative right exists then no common stock dividends may be paid until all preferred dividends in arrears have been paid.
Right to share in additional dividends	This right only exists if preferred stock is participating	The right to share in excess dividends may exist, if so, it is called the *participating* right. Assume that the board of directors declares a dividend that is large enough to (1) pay the stated percentage

		dividend to preferred stockholders, (2) a like percentage dividend to common stockholders and (3) after paying both dividends an excess dividend exists. If the preferred stock is *participating* the then excess dividend will be divided, pro rata, between the common and preferred stockholders.

Another example . . . let's assume that a corporation has the following capital structure:

1. 100,000 shares of $1.00 par common stock are authorized.
2. 20,000 shares of $15.00 par 10% preferred stock are authorized (the preferred shares holders are entitled to a 10 percent, or $1.50, per share dividend.
3. 50,000 shares of common stock have been sold at an average price of $12.00 per share and 45,000 shares are currently outstanding.
4. 10,000 shares of preferred stock have been sold at an average price of $20.00 per share.
5. 5,000 shares of common stock treasury stock were purchased by the corporation for $15.00 per share.

What would the owners' equity section of the balance sheet look like? Try again, and then check in the box on the following page.

Preferred stock, $15 par, 10%, 20,000 shares authorized, 10,000 shares issued and outstanding	$ 150,000
Common stock, $1 par, 100,000 shares authorized, 50,000 shares issued, 45,000 shares outstanding	$ 50,000
Paid-in capital in excess of par – Preferred	$ 50,000
Paid-in capital in excess of par – Common	$ 550,000
Treasury Stock	($ 75,000)

The last item that you will usually find in the stockholders' equity section of the balance sheet is *retained earnings*. Retained earnings represents cumulative, undistributed net income. That is, it is the total of net income earned since the inception of the corporation less any amounts distributed to stockholders as dividends or reallocated to other accounts.

If we assume that a corporation had retained earnings of $100,000 at the beginning of the year, that it earned net income of $75,000 and paid dividends totaling $25,000 to its stockholders then retained earnings reported on the balance sheet at the end of the year would be calculated as:

Retained earnings, beginning of year	$100,000
Add, net income	$ 75,000
Less, dividends	($ 25,000)
Retained earnings, end of year	$ 150,000

Now with this background, let's take a look at a more complex balance sheet in Figure 2.7.

Figure 2.7
Classified Balance Sheet

ABC Corporation
Balance Sheet
December 31, 2013

Assets
  Current Assets

Cash	$100,000	
Marketable Securities	25,000	
Accounts Receivable	75,000	
Inventory	300,000	
Prepaid Expenses	20,000	
Total Current Assets		$ 520,000

Property, Plant and Equipment

Land	$150,000	
Buildings	$700,000	
Less Accumulated Depreciation	(200,000)	500,000
Equipment	$800,000	
Less Accumulated Depreciation	(150,000)	650,000
Total Property, Plant and Equipment		$1,300,000

Intangible Assets

Patents, less amortization	$ 50,000	
Trademarks, less amortization	25,000	
Total Intangible Assets		75,000
Total Assets		$1,895,000

Total Liabilities and Equity
  Liabilities
  Current Liabilities

Accounts Payable	$ 150,000	
Current Portion of Long-term Debt	80,000	
Wages Payable	50,000	
Taxes Payable	15,000	
Total Current Liabilities		$ 295,000

Long-term Liabilities		
Mortgage Payable	$ 600,000	
Bond Payable	100,000	
Total Long-term Liabilities		700,000
Total Liabilities		$ 995,000
Stockholders' Equity		
Common Stock, $1 par, 100,000 shares authorized		
80,000 shares issued and outstanding	$ 80,000	
Paid-in Capital in Excess of Par	460,000	
Treasury Stock	(40,000)	
Retained Earnings	400,000	
Total Stockholders' Equity		900,000
Total Liabilities and Stockholders' Equity		$ 1,895,000

Some of the line items on this sample balance sheet may look unfamiliar to you. Don't worry; we will address them in subsequent chapters. For now just make sure that you are familiar with the structure of the balance sheet and the major sections with in it.

Conclusion

We took our first look at the balance sheet in this chapter. You now know that the accounting equation is reflected in the balance sheet and you know the major account classifications on a balance sheet. In addition, you know that the balance sheet shows a picture of a company's financial position at a point in time; and that "financial position" to an accountant is not the same as the current market value or market cap of a company.

Among other things, balance sheets are useful for assessing liquidity and the use of leverage. Financial statements tell stories and numbers talk. Now that you understand the basic format of a balance sheet and have learned a few tools for analyzing liquidity and leverage, the balance sheet has started to talk to you. In the next chapter we will begin to see how the balance sheet and the income statement can be used together to evaluate how well a company is managing key assets.

Appendix 2.1

Recording Balance Sheet Transactions in Tabular Format

In this chapter we looked at the effect of the Kid's Klothes' start-up transactions on their balance sheet. These transactions were:

1. The owner invested $10,000 in the corporation in exchange for common stock,
2. The business borrowed $20,000 on a short-term line of credit,
3. Kid's Klothes purchased store furniture and fixtures for $8,000 and paid cash, and
4. The business purchased inventory for $10,000 and paid cash.

One way that accountants could record these transactions is to use a table with one column for each account. Years ago many small business used a similar system, call the One Write ® system that let them write checks and record transactions on a table at the same time.

By reviewing the transactions above we can quickly identify the types of accounts that we will need in our table. Let's organize the accounts by account type (asset, liability, equity) as in the accounting equation. When we do this we have the following list of accounts:

- Assets
  - o Cash
  - o Inventory
  - o Store Equipment
- Liabilities
  - o Short-term note payable
- Equity
  - o Common stock

42

Now we can build a transaction table and use it to record the transactions:

Figure A2.1.1
Transaction Table

Tran	Assets			Liabilities	Equity
	Cash	Inventory	Store Equipment	Short-term Note	Common Stock
1					
2					
3					
4					
Totals					

Let's record the first transaction, the owner's $10,000 investment in exchange for common stock. This transaction increases the cash balance by $10,000 and also increases the balance in the equity account, common stock. Note that after we record the transaction below the accounting equation is still in balance because assets ($10,000) are equal to liabilities ($-0-) plus equity ($10,000).

Figure A2.1.2
Transaction Table – Transaction 1

Tran	Assets			Liabilities	Owners' Equity
	Cash	Inventory	Store Equipment	Short-term Note	Common Stock
1	10,000				10,000
2					
3					
4					
Totals	10,000				10,000

In the second transaction the business borrowed $20,000 from the bank. This transaction increased the asset cash by $20,000 and also increased the liability, short-term note payable, by the same amount. Like the first transaction, this is an asset source transaction, a transaction that provided assets the company could use. Look at the total line below to check and make sure that the accounting equation (Assets = Liabilities + Owners' Equity) is still in balance.

Figure A2.1.3
Transaction Table – Transaction 2

Tran	Assets			Liabilities	Owners' Equity
	Cash	Inventory	Store Equipment	Short-term Note	Common Stock
1	10,000				10,000
2	20,000			20,000	
3					
4					
Totals	30,000			20,000	10,000

The third transaction was an asset exchange transaction. That means that one asset, cash in this case, was exchanged for another, store equipment. The total asset amount should remain unchanged because we are increasing the balance in one asset account and reducing the asset balance in another by the same amount. Let's see how the purchase of store equipment for $8,000 would be recorded. Again, after recording the transaction check to make sure that the accounting equation is still in balance.

Figure A2.1.4
Transaction Table – Transaction 3

Tran	Assets			Liabilities	Owners' Equity
	Cash	Inventory	Store Equipment	Short-term Note	Common Stock
1	10,000				10,000
2	20,000			20,000	
3	(8,000)		8,000		
4					
Totals	22,000		8,000	20,000	10,000

Well, is the accounting equation still in balance? Of course it is; that is the beauty of double entry accounting. Total assets equal $30,000, the same as the sum of liabilities and owners' equity. It's just that now we have two asset accounts.

The purchase of inventory for $10,000 in cash was another asset exchange transaction. See if you can visualize how it would be recorded before you look at the table below.

Figure A2.1.5
Transaction Table – Transaction 4

Tran	Assets			Liabilities	Owners' Equity
	Cash	Inventory	Store Equipment	Short-term Note	Common Stock
1	10,000				10,000
2	20,000			20,000	
3	(8,000)		8,000		
4	(10,000)	10,000			
Totals	12,000	10,000	8,000	20,000	10,000

The balances on the total line of the table above should look familiar. They are the same balances as were recorded on the balance sheet that we looked at in this chapter. The balance sheet is reproduced below. It might be a good idea to compare the table above with the balance sheet so you can see how the two tie together.

Figure A2.1.6
Kids' Klothes Balance Sheet

Kids' Klothes
Balance Sheet
June 30, 2013

Assets
    Current Assets
        Cash $12,000
        Inventory   10,000
        Total Current Assets $22,000

    Property, Plant & Equipment
        Store Fixtures $ 8,000
        Total Property, Plant & Equipment   8,000

Total Assets
    $30,000

Liabilities and Owner's Equity
Liabilities
    Current Liabilities
        Short-term line of credit $20,000
Total Liabilities $20,000

Owner's Equity
    Common Stock $10,000
Total Owner's Equity   10,000

Total Liabilities and Owner's Equity $30,000

Appendix 2.2

Debits and Credits

Businesses could use a table like the one that you saw in Appendix 2.2 to record all of their transactions. In fact, it would be easy to set up a worksheet on a computer to do exactly that. The only problem with that is that the table would become extremely large. Just imagine how many different assets, liability and owners' equity accounts a major corporation like GM or Walmart would have. Then think about how many rows the table would have if each business transaction required just one row.

In practice business transactions are recorded in journal entries. A journal entry records the increases and decreases to the accounts affected by a transaction. Recall the owner investment transaction. Both cash and the common stock accounts were increased by that transaction. The journal entry for that transaction would then include entries to increase the cash account balance and to increase the equity account, common stock. That is done with debits and credits.

Let's place the accounting equation over a T as shown in the figure below in Figure A2-2.1.

Figure A2.2.1
T Representation

ASSETS =   LIABILITES + OWNERS'
EQUITY

Accountants have agreed to call the left side of the "T" the "debit" side and to call the right side of the "T" the "credit" side. All that debit and credit mean are *left* and *right*. Debits don't have personalities, they are not good or bad, desirable or undesirable, debits just mean left and credits just mean right[1].

Debit and credit take on more meaning when they are used in conjunction with a specific account in the double entry system. Figure A2.2.2 illustrates the different operations that could be performed while maintaining the equality of the accounting equation (+ = increase, - = decrease) using the same "T" format.

Figure A2.2.2
Accounting Operations

ASSETS = LIABILITES + OWNERS' EQUITY

1.	+	+
2.	-	-
3.	±	
4.		±

As you can see in Figure A2.2.2, our goal is make sure that the accounting equation is always in balance, that is that the left side (assets) is always equal to the right side (liabilities + owners' equity). There are only four possible operations. In the first case we can increase both the left and right sides of the equation by the same amount. The owner of Kids Klothes' investment of

[1] Debit come from comes from the Latin debitum, "that which is owing" and was first used in double-entry book-keeping in Medieval Venice. Credit, on the other hand, comes from Credo or to believe or to trust. It is in the 3rd person so it would be translated directly into English as He/She/It believes or trusts.

$10,000 in cash in exchange for common stock was an example of that type of operation or transaction.

As in case 2 above, we can decrease the left and right sides of the equation by the same amount. For example, recall that Kids Klothes borrowed $20,000 from the bank. If they were to pay $1,000 of that loan back to the bank we would reduce assets (cash) by $1,000 and reduce the liability short-term note payable by the same amount. Kids Klothes would have $1,000 less cash, but at the same time it would now only owe $19,000 to the bank.

The third type of transaction illustrated above is an asset exchange transactions. In these transactions one asset, often cash, is exchanged for another asset. Both the purchase of store fixtures and the purchase of inventory were examples of this type of transaction. These transactions only affect the left side (asset side) of the accounting equation leaving total assets unchanged.

Finally in the fourth type of transaction one liability or equity account is exchanged for another. For example, what would happen if Kids Klothes decided that it couldn't pay the short-term loan back on time and the bank agreed to exchange the amount owed on the short-term note for a five-year, long-term note payable. We would reduce the amount in the short-term note payable account and increase the balance (amount) in the new long-term note payable account.

Rather than saying "plus" or "minus", or even "increase " or "decrease" accountants use the words "debit" and "credit" to explain how the balance in an account is affected by a transaction. Table A2.3 below shows how debits and credits are used with specific account types.

50

Figure A2.2.3
Debits and Credits

ASSETS = LIABILITES + OWNERS' EQUITY

| *Increase* | Debit | Credit |
| *Decrease* | Credit | Debit |

Double entry accounting requires that every transaction be recorded in at least two accounts. It also requires that debits equal credits in every transaction. Earlier we learned that today "debit" only means "left". Assets are on the left side of the accounting equation by convention and so debits are used to increase asset account balances. One way to maintain the equality of the accounting equation was to increase the balance on the liability and equity side of the equation when we increased the balance on the asset side. If debits are used to increase assets, and every transaction requires both at least one debit and one credit, then we have to use credits to increase balances on the right side of the accounting equation. If debits increase assets, then we have to use credits to decrease assets. By the same token, if credits increase liability and equity accounts then debits must be used to decrease them.

The following table uses debits and credits to record the four transactions that we recorded in a table in Appendix 2.1. Note in the journal entry form below that debits are recorded on the left and that credits are recorded on the right (and that credit account titles are indented a little to the right as well).

Every journal entry has five parts:

1.	Transaction date, or number in this case,
2.	Accounts affected by the transaction,
3.	At least one debit,
4.	At least one credit, and
5.	A description of the transaction.

Figure A2.2.4
Journal Entries

Transaction	Account	Debit	Credit
1	Cash	10,000	
	Common Stock		10,000
	To record the owners'		
	investment of $10,000 in		
	exchange for common stock		
2	Cash	10,000	
	Short-term Note Payable		10,000
	To record a short-term bank		
	loan taken out by Kids		
	Klothes.		
3	Store Fixtures	8,000	
	Cash		8,000
	To record the purchase of		
	store fixtures for cash.		
4	Inventory	10,000	
	Cash		10,000
	To record the purchase of		
	store inventory for cash.		

Transactions are always recorded in chronological order in journal entries. The book in which transactions are recorded is called the "General Journal". It doesn't matter if a company uses a manual accounting system or a computer-based accounting system. The book of original entry, the general journal, always shows the transactions in chronological order. The transaction description may seem redundant because it really doesn't tell you anything that you can't learn by reading the debits and credits. However, in practice the description includes reference numbers to source documents. The reference numbers include things like check numbers, invoice numbers, purchase order numbers, etc. The recording of these reference numbers makes it possible to work backwards from journal entries to the original business documents. A journal entry summarizes the accounting effect of a business event, but it doesn't tell us everything we might want to know about a business transaction; for that we may need to review the original source document.

Chapter 3
Did I Earn a Profit? – The Income Statement

When you can measure what you are speaking about, and express it in numbers, you know something about it, but if you cannot measure it, when you cannot express it in numbers, your knowledge is of a meager and unsatisfactory kind.

– Lord Kelvin (1883)

Well, I think we are doing ok, but some numbers would be nice.

The Income Statement

In the last chapter we looked at the balance sheet. Recall that the balance sheet provides a picture of a company's financial position *at a point in time*. The income statement tells whether the company operated at a profit or loss over *a period of time*. An income statement can be prepared for a month, a quarter, a year or any other period of time that is of interest to decision makers. The income statement shows the results of operations over that period of time. Net income, or the results of operations, is computed as:

$$Net\ Income = Revenues - Expenses + Gains - Losses$$

Revenues represent the amount that a company has earned from normal business operations. Gains, like revenues, increase net income; however gains result from events and transaction that are outside the normal scope of business operations. Remember Kids' Klothes from Chapter 2? The owner purchased $8,000 of store furniture and fixtures in the last chapter. Let's assume that the owner then decided that one of the rounds (the round rack from which clothes are hung) didn't fit well within the store. The round cost $800 and had never been used. The owner sold the round for $1,000 to a friend who really needed it in her gym (she had decided to try to sell exercise clothing to her gym members). Kids' Klothes is in business to sell children's clothing and not store fixtures. The sale of the round is outside the normal scope of business operations. Because the round sold for more than its net book value (historical cost less accumulated depreciation) so Kids' Klothes would recognize a gain on the sale. Note that accumulated depreciation is the sum, over time, of depreciation expense. If a company recorded depreciation expense of $500 per year on an asset for three years then at the end of the three years accumulated depreciation would total $1,500. We will look at depreciation in detail in Chapter Six.

Expenses are the ordinary and necessary costs of doing business. For Kids' Clothes expenses would include rent, utilities, advertising, employee salaries, and of course the cost of the clothing that is sold. Had Kids' Klothes sold the $800 round for $750 then it would have reported a $50 loss on the sale, not a

$50 business expense.   Again, because losses resulted from ancillary transactions.

Let's assume that in the first month of operations Kids' Klothes sold inventory costing $5,000 for $9.000.   It also paid store rent of $1,000, advertising expenses of $400, utilities (electricity, telephone and water) of $300, and interest of $100 on its bank loan. Don't forget that store fixtures costing $8,000 were purchased and that one round that cost $800 was sold for $1,000. Did the owner make a profit? The income statement in Figure 3.1 will answer that question for us.

Figure 3.1
Income Statement

Kids' Klothes
Income Statement
For the Month Ended July 31, 2013

Revenue	$ 9,000	
Cost of Goods Sold	(5,000)	
Gross Profit		$ 4,000
Operating Expenses		
Rent	($ 1,000)	
Advertising	(400)	
Utilities	(300)	
Total Operating Expenses		(1,700)
Income from Operations		$ 2,300
Other Income & Expenses		
Gain on Sale of Store Fixtures	$ 200	
Interest Expense	(100)	
Total Other Income		100
Income Before Taxes		$ 2,400
Income Tax Expense		(720)
Net Income		$ 1,680

Remember the question? Did Kids' Klothes make a profit in its first month of operations? The answer is "yes". Revenues were greater than expenses so the company reported net income, not a net loss.

There are a couple of things we should note about the income statement. First, it is dated for a period of time, in this case the month of July, and not as of a specific date like the balance sheet. The Kids' Klothes income statement reports on the results of operations for the month of July; it summarizes everything that happened in July, just like the score of a football game.

Notice too that accountants us brackets to rather than minus signs when they subtract. I guess we are afraid that a little minus sign might get lost in all the numbers. Often however, when subtraction is assumed to be obvious the brackets are omitted. This is often the case in the first section of the income statement. Finally, notice that the income statement is divided into a few different sections. We are going to analyze each section in detail.

Gross Profit

Let's take a closer look at what is going on in the first section, the gross profit section.

Revenue	$ 9,000
Cost of Goods Sold	(5,000)
Gross Profit	$ 4,000

The cost of inventory that is sold by a business is an expense. However, because it is the most significant expense for a retail or manufacturing company it is usually shown in a separate section. This also makes it easy to compute the gross profit or gross margin.

$$Gross\ Profit = Revenue - Cost\ of\ Goods\ Sold$$

Gross profit is the difference between the selling price and the cost of inventory. It is the sum that is left, after covering the cost of inventory that was sold, to pay all of the other expenses and to provide a profit. Owners and managers pay close attention to this number and to the cost of goods sold and gross profit percentages.

$$Cost\ of\ Goods\ Sold\ Percentage = \frac{Cost\ of\ Goods\ Sold}{Sales}\ x\ 100$$

$$Gross\ Profit\ Percentage = \frac{Gross\ Profit}{Sales}\ x\ 100$$

The gross profit percentage tells you how much is left out of every sales dollar to cover expenses and provide profit. For Kids' Clothes these metrics are:

$$Cost\ of\ Goods\ Sold\ Percentage = \frac{\$5,000}{\$9,000}\ x\ 100 = 56\%$$

and

$$Gross\ Profit\ Percentage = \frac{\$4,000}{\$9,000}\ x\ 100 = 44\%$$

This means that 56 percent of every sales dollar at Kids' Klothes goes to cover the cost of the inventory that was sold, leaving 44 percent (or 44 cents out of every sales dollar) to cover all of the other business expenses and to provide a profit.

Now let's compare Walmart and Target using information from their 2012 income statements. Figure 3.2 below summarizes their cost of goods sold sections (ignoring credit card revenue and expenses). Note that all amounts are in millions of dollars.

Figure 3.2
Comparative Income Statements

	Walmart	Target
Revenue	$443,854	$ 68,466
Cost of Goods Sold	335,127	47,860
Gross Profit	$108,727	$ 20,606

So, which company generated more gross profit from each sale? It's hard to tell looking at the dollar amounts. However if we compute the gross profit percentages we can get a better feel for what is going on.

$$Walmart\ Gross\ Profit\ Percentage = \frac{\$108,727}{\$443,854}\ x\ 100 = 24.5\%$$

$$Target\ Gross\ Profit\ Percentage = \frac{\$20,606}{\$68,466}\ x\ 100 = 30.4\%$$

Walmart generates more gross profit *dollars* than Target. That is because it is considerably bigger than Target. However, Target has a higher gross profit *percentage*. Target's higher gross profit percentage could result from lower cost of goods sold, that is Target pays less for its inventory than does Walmart. Conversely it could also result from higher prices, a higher markup on cost, than that of Walmart. If you have shopped at both stores, which do you think it is?

Operating Expenses

We find ordinary and necessary business expenses in the second section of the income statement. This section for Kids' Klothes showed the following:

Operating Expenses		
Rent	($ 1,000)	
Advertising	(400)	
Utilities	(300)	
Total Operating Expenses		($ 1,700)

Other expenses that you would expect to find in this section include salary and wages expenses and depreciation expense. Depreciation will be discussed in depth in Chapter 6. For now think of depreciation as the systematic assignment of the cost of fixed assets, things like buildings and equipment, to the time periods that benefit from the use of the assets. Other common expenses that are included in the operating expenses section of an income statement are research and development cost, restructuring costs, and general, selling and administrative costs.

Figure 3.3 compares the cost of goods sold and operating expenses sections of Walmart and Target's January 30, 2012 annual income statements.

Figure 3.3
Walmart and Target
Comparative Income Statements
For the Year-ended January, 2012
(All Amounts in Millions)

	Walmart	Target
Total Revenue	$446,950	$69,865
Less Cost of Goods Sold	335,127	47,860
Gross Profit	$111,823	$22,005
Less Operating Expenses		
Selling, General & Administrative	85,265	14,552
Other		2,131
Income from Operations	$ 26,558	$ 5,322

Once again it is hard to tell, looking at the dollar amounts, whether Walmart or Target is doing a better job managing its costs. When we want to compare companies that are very different in size it helps to convert the financial statements to common sized financial statements. A common sized financial statement shows all amounts as percentages. A common sized income statement shows all amounts as a percentage of sales (all dollar amounts are divided by total sales to convert to percentages). The common-sized statements for Walmart and Target are shown in Figure 3.4 below.

Figure 3.4
Comparative Common-Sized Income Statements
For the Year-ended January, 2012
(All Amounts in Millions)

	Walmart	Target
Total Revenue	100.0%	100.0%
Less Cost of Goods Sold	75.0	68.5
Gross Profit	25.0%	31.5%
Less Operating Expenses		
Selling, General & Administrative	19.1	20.8
Other		3.1
Income from Operations	5.9%	7.6%

Now we can start to draw some comparative conclusions about Walmart and Target. Note again that Target has a higher gross profit percentage than does Walmart, probably from higher mark-ups (prices), but they lose some of that advantage because they also have higher operating expenses as a percentage of sales.

In addition to preparing common-sized income statements to compare different companies you can also use them to see how a company has changed over time. For example, Target's gross profit percentage (gross profit divided by sales) has decreased from 32.6 percent in 2010 to 32.1 percent in 2011 to 31.5 percent in 2012. What might cause such a change? Could it be that Target has been responding to competitive pressure by reducing prices?

Revenue Recognition and Matching

Remember accrual accounting from Chapter 1? Probably not, because I didn't call it that in Chapter 1. What you did learn in Chapter 1 was that there are specific rules for revenue recognition and expense matching. These are the rules of accrual accounting. In accrual accounting revenues are reported on the income statement when a company has earned the right to get paid and not when payment is actually received. Expenses are reported, or recognized, when a company incurs the obligation to pay the expenses and not when the checks to pay the expenses are written. For example, assume that the pizza parlor accepted an invitation to cater a party. The party was held on June 25th and everyone who attended the party raved about the gourmet pizzas. At the end of the party the manager of the pizza parlor presented the host with a bill for $1,500. The host wrote a check and mailed it to the pizza parlor on July 2nd. Should the $1,500 of party revenue be reported as June or July revenue?

The pizza parlor uses accrual accounting and it earned the right to get paid when it catered the party on June 25th (we say that the earnings process was complete when the party was catered). That means that the $1,500 is June revenue even though payment was not received until July 2nd. The $1,500 would be included on the June income statement. Not only that, but all of the expenses related to the party should be reported as June expenses as well. The party-related expenses must be *matched* with the revenue from the party in the same accounting period (the month of June). This is the *matching principle*. It doesn't matter when the expenses were paid, the costs were incurred in June so they should be included on the June income statement.

Other Income and Expenses

The other income and expense section of an income statement shows income and expenses from non-operating activities. The most common items included in this section are interest income and expense, and gains and losses from the sale of assets. Lending and borrowing activities, the activities that result in interest income and expense, are not the primary business activities of most business so the income and expenses from these activities are reported in this section. The other income and expense section for Kids' Klothes showed:

Other Income & Expenses
    Gain on Sale of Store Fixtures $ 200
        Interest Expense   (100)
Total Other Income $ 100

Recall that Kids' Klothes sold a round, but that they are not in the business of selling store fixtures, so the gain on the sale was not included in income from operations.

One other item is reported separately on financial statements. This item is so important that they are reported after income from continuing operations. This item is the sale or disposal of a segment of the business This event is not expected of occur frequently and so it is not expected to affect the income statements of future periods. Income or loss from discontinued operations is disclosed net of taxes, that is, after adjusting for the tax effect of the items.

When a business decides to sell a division or other segment the operating income or loss from that segment, along with any gain or loss on the sale, are reported as a separate line item on the income statement. Current operating income is usually believed to be the best indicator of future income. The division or segment that is sold or closed will not exist in the future and so it is shown separately so that users of the income statement can accurately forecast future net income.

Assume that a company had income from continuing operations of $1.5 million and that they had decided to sell an unprofitable division. The unprofitable division had an operating loss of $500,000 and was sold for a loss of $300,000. The company has an income tax rate of 30 percent. The company's income statement would show:

Income from continuing operations (before taxes)	$1,500,000
Loss from discontinued operations, net of a $240,000 tax benefit	($ 560,000)
Income before taxes	$ 940,000
Less Income Tax Expense	(210,000)
Net Income	$ 730,000

The $800,000 loss (the $500,000 operating loss and the $300,000 loss on the sale) reduced taxable income and consequently also reduced taxes by $240,000, ($800,000 x 0.30) the amount of the "tax benefit". The loss is shown net of the tax benefit ($560,000 = $800,000 - $240,000).

Prior to December 15, 2015 FASB required the additional disclosure of extraordinary items, again net of taxes. An extraordinary item was defined as an event that resulted in a gain or a loss that is (1) unusual in nature and (2) infrequent in occurrence. An event had to meet *both* criteria before it could be separately reported on an income statement. For example, the loss from frost damage to the citrus crop in Florida would not be considered to be an extraordinary item because it is neither unusual or infrequent, neither would tornado damage to a warehouse in Tusla. However, if a tornado damaged a warehouse in Maine that loss would most likely be classified as extraordinary because tornados are both unusual in nature and infrequent in occurrence in Maine.

Extraordinary items occurred so infrequently that FASB, in Accounting Standards Update No. 2015-01, *Income Statement—Extraordinary and Unusual Items (Subtopic 225-20), Simplifying Income Statement Presentation by Eliminating the Concept of Extraordinary Items*, decided to eliminate the disclosure because of the cost and effort needed to report these infrequent items.

Income Taxes

Income taxes are the last item deducted on an income statement. You might be curious about the $210,000 income tax expense reported on the partial income statement above. It was calculated as follows:

Income from continuing operations (before taxes)	$1,500,000
Times the tax rate	x .30
Preliminary Income Tax Expens	$ 450,000
Less Tax Benefit from Discontinued Operation	(240,000)
Income Tax Expense	$ 210,000

There is usually a difference between income tax expense on the income statement and the amount of tax that a business actually pays to the federal government. This results from differences between generally accepted accounting principles (GAAP) and the tax code. The two do not measure revenues and expenses the same way. These differences result in both temporary or timing differences and permanent differences between income tax expense and income tax liability.

For example, because of the matching principle a business will record expected warranty expense when a sale is made and will base that expense on historical warranty claims. This amount will be reported on the income statement as an expense. However, the income tax code only permits the deduction of warranty expenses when the expenses are actually paid. This difference is a timing difference because the warranty expense is deductible in both case, but may not be deducted on the income statement and tax return in the same year.

On the other hand, if you invest in state or municipal bonds you probably know that the interest on those bonds is tax exempt, that is, it will never be included in taxable income. However, the interest earned would be included in income for financial reporting purposes. Because this interest is reported on an income statement but will never be taxed on a tax return interest from state and municipal bonds results in a permanent difference between financial statement net income and taxable income.

Other differences between financial statement net income and taxable income are temporary. They result because the tax code and GAAP have different revenue recognition and expense matching rules. For example, under GAAP companies are required to estimate the future cost of repairs and replacements that they might make when goods are sold with a warranty. That means that under GAAP a company records an estimated warranty expense when a product is sold. The tax code, on the other hand, requires that warranty expense be recorded as a tax-deductible expense when the warranty costs are actually paid. The effects of temporary timing differences are reported on the balance sheet as deferred tax assets and deferred tax liabilities. This means that if a company sold a product in 2015 with an estimated future warranty expense of $40 and then paid the repair costs under warranty in 2016 that it would record the $40 of warranty expense on its 2015 income statement, but would not include the expense on its 2015 tax return. The tax deduction would have to wait until the 2016 tax return was prepared because the cost was paid in 2016.

Profitability Analysis

While net income is the primary tool used to measure profitability some other measures are used as well. Key measures that you should understand are the gross profit or gross margin percentage, profit margin, and earnings per share.

You already know how to compute the gross profit or gross margin percentage:

$$Gross\ Profit\ Percentage = \frac{Gross\ Profit}{Sales}\ x\ 100$$

Profit margin is computed as:

$$Profit\ Margin = \frac{Net\ Income}{Sales}\ x\ 100$$

Recall that Kids' Klothes had sales of $9,000 and net income of $1,680 after the first month of operations. Consequently its profit margin was:

$$Profit\ Margin = \frac{\$1,680}{\$9,000}\ x\ 100 = 18.7\%$$

Profit margin shows the percentage of every sales dollar that is left to provide a profit. Another way to think of it is that for every dollar in sales made by Kids' Klothes they can expect 18.7 cents of profit. The profit margins for Walmart (5.9 percent) and Target (7.6 percent) were computed on the comparative common-sized income statements shown above.

Earnings per Share

Earnings per Share (EPS) is a measure of the net income earned by or attributable to every share of common stock. It is one of the most common and important profitability measures. It is also one of the most important factors used to estimate stock prices and is used to compute the price/earnings (P/E) ratio. Finally, securities analysts usually forecast companies EPS numbers so if you are looking at a publicly traded company you can probably find securities analysts' profitability projections.

When a company only has one class of stock, usually called "common stock", and the number of shares of stock outstanding during the period (a month or a year for example) didn't change over the course of the reporting period earnings per share is computed as:

$$Basic\ Earnings\ Per\ Share = \frac{Net\ Income}{Number\ of\ Share\ of\ Common\ Stock}$$

Let's assume that Kids' Klothes is a closely held corporation. In fact, let's assume that the owner of Kids' Klothes owns all 1,000 share of common stock that the company has issued. If that is the case then EPS for the month of July would be computed as:

$$Basic\ Earnings\ Per\ Share = \frac{Net\ Income}{Number\ of\ Share\ of\ Common\ Stock}$$
$$= \frac{\$1,680}{1000\ shares} = \$1.68\ per\ share$$

On January 31, 2013 and Walmart and Target's basic EPS were $4.86 and $4.51 per share respectively. As of January 2, 2013 securities analysts were forecasting year-end (January 31, 2013) EPS for Walmart and Target of $4.92 and $4.40 per share respectively. This means that Target exceeded analysts' expectations while Walmart fell short.

Conclusion

The income statement tells us whether or not a company made a profit. It can also give us an idea of the cost structure of a business. For example, we can see how much of every sales dollar went to cover the cost of inventory sold, for normal operating expenses, and even for interest payments and taxes. In addition, we can compare the cost structures of different companies using common-sized income statements.

Most companies prepare their financial statements using accrual accounting so the income statement shows revenue earned and expenses incurred. It doesn't show us how much cash was collected from customers, how the cash was spent, and how much cash is left at the end of a period. That's the job of the cash flow statement.

You will learn how to read and understand the cash flow statement in the next chapter. In chapter 5 we will take a more in-depth look at how to analyze financial statements.

Appendix 3.1
Recording Income Statement Transactions in Tabular Format

In Appendix 2.1 we learned how to record balance sheet transactions in tabular form. In this appendix we will learn how to record income statement (revenue and expense) transactions in tabular format. To do that we will need to expand our table so that it includes columns for revenues and expenses (see Table A3.1.1 below).

Table A3.1.1
Transaction Table

Tran	Assets			Lia.	Equity		Income Statement		
No.	Cash	Inventory	Store Equipment	Short-Term Note	Common Stock	Retained Earnings	Rev.	Exp.	Gain
Beg.	12,000	10,000	8,000	20,000	10,000				

Revenue and expense accounts (and gain and loss accounts as well) are call *temporary accounts* because, unlike balance sheet accounts, the income statement accounts are closed into owners' equity at the end of an accounting period. When accountants say that an account has been "closed" they mean that the balance in the account has be transferred to another account leaving the original account with a zero balance. By the way, balance sheet accounts are call *permanent* accounts. The balances at the beginning of the month ("Beg." in Table 3-1.1) were carried forward from the end of the previous month. These accounts with balanced that are carried forward from one period to another are the *permanent accounts*.

Because revenue and expense accounts are really part of owners' equity an increase in revenue *increases* equity and an increase in expenses *decreases* owners' equity. Let's see how this works with the Kids' Klothes transactions for the first month of operations. The transactions for the month were:

1. Kids' Klothes sold inventory costing $5,000 for $9.000 in cash,
2. Paid store rent of $1,000,
3. Paid advertising expenses of $400,
4. Paid utilities (electricity, telephone and water) of $300, and
5. Paid interest of $100 on its bank loan.
6. Kids' Klothes also sold a store fixture that cost $800 for $1,000, a $200 gain on the sale.
7. We will ignore taxes in this illustration.

Table A3.1.2
Transaction Table

Tran No.	Assets			Lia.	Equity		Income Statement		
	Cash	Inv.	Store Equip	Short-Term Note	Common Stock	Retained Earnings	Rev.	Exp.	Gain
Beg.	12,000	10,000	8,000	20,000	10,000				
1a	9,000						9,000		
1b		-5,000						5,000	
2	-1,000							1,000	
3	-400							400	
4	-300							300	
5	-100							100	
6									
Total									

Notice that transaction one required two entries in the table. Transaction 1a recorded the receipt of cash and the recognition of revenue earned. The second part of the transaction recorded the reduction of inventory, for the cost of inventory sold, and an increase in expenses for the cost of the goods that were sold (which will reduce retained earnings in the equity section).

Transactions two through five were cash payments for various expenses. These four transactions resulted in decreases in the cash account and increases in the expense account (resulting in an eventual decrease in retained earnings). In practice accountants would use a separate expense account (column) for each expense category.

The final transaction was the sale of a store fixture for cash. Table A3-1.3 shows how this transaction would be recorded. Notice that this transaction was recorded in three columns and that cash received is equal to the cost of the store fixture sold and the gain on the sale. Another way to view this is that the selling price minus cost is equal to gain.

It would be a good idea now to see if the accounting equation is still in balance. At first glance it might look like we have a problem because obviously assets ($32,400) are not equal to the sum of liabilities ($20,000) and equity ($10,000). However the temporary accounts (revenues, expenses and gain in this case) are really equity accounts (retained earnings) as well. Net income (revenue – expenses + gains) is equal to $2,400 ($9,000 - $6,800 + $200). When we include the temporary account totals in our calculation of liabilities plus equity then assets ($32,400) are equal to liabilities plus equity ($20,000 + $10,000 + $2,400).

Table A3.1.3
Transaction Table

Tran No.	Assets			Lia.	Equity		Income Statement		
	Cash	Inv.	Store Equip	Short-Term Note	Common Stock	Retained Earnings	Rev.	Exp.	Gain
Beg.	12,000	10,000	8,000	20,000	10,000				
1a	9,000						9,000		
1b		-5,000						5,000	
2	-1,000							1,000	
3	-400							400	
4	-300							300	
5	-100							100	
6	1,000		-800						200
Total	20,200	5,000	7,200	20,000	10,000		9,000	6,800	200

Now that we have the account balances (totals) for the month we can use these balances to prepare an income statement (see Figure A3.2.1 below).

Figure A3.2.1
Income Statement

Kids' Klothes
Income Statement
For the Month Ended July 31, 2013

Revenue	$ 9,000	
Cost of Goods Sold	(5,000)	
Gross Profit		$ 4,000
Operating Expenses		
Rent	($ 1,000)	
Advertising	(400)	
Utilities	(300)	
Total Operating Expenses		(1,700)
Income from Operations		$ 2,300
Other Income & Expenses		
Gain on Sale of Store Fixtures	$ 200	
Interest Expense	(100)	
Total Other Income		100
Income Before Taxes		$ 2,400

The last thing that happens at the end of an accounting period is that the temporary accounts are closed into retained earnings. The closing process transfers the balances in those accounts from the temporary accounts to retained earnings. Table A3.1.5 shows how this is done.

Table A3.1.5
Transaction Table

	Assets			Lia.	Equity		Income Statement		
Tran No.	Cash	Inv.	Store Equip	Short-Term Note	Common Stock	Retained Earnings	Rev.	Exp.	Gain
Beg.	12,000	10,000	8,000	20,000	10,000				
1a	9,000						9,000		
1b		-5,000						5,000	
2	-1,000							1,000	
3	-400							400	
4	-300							300	
5	-100							100	
6	1,000		-800						200
Total	20,200	5,000	7,200	20,000	10,000		9,000	6,800	200
Close						2,400	-9,000	-6,800	-200
Total	20,000	5,000	7,200	20,000	10,000	2,400	0	0	0

Notice, in the highlighted row in Table A3.2.5 that the balances in the temporary accounts are subtracted from the respective accounts and the total is transferred to retained earnings. Now it should be more obvious that the accounting equation balances. However, just to make sure, let's prepare a month-end balance sheet (Figure A3.1.2)

Figure A3.1.2
Kids' Klothes Balance Sheet

Kids' Klothes
Balance Sheet
July 31, 2013

Assets
    Current Assets
        Cash $20,200
        Inventory   5,000
    Total Current Assets $25,200
    Property, Plant & Equipment
        Store Fixtures $ 7,200
    Total Property, Plant & Equipment   7,200
Total Assets $32,400

Liabilities and Owner's Equity
Liabilities
    Current Liabilities
        Short-term line of credit $20,000
Total Liabilities $20,000
Owner's Equity
    Common Stock $10,000
    Retained Earnings   2,400
Total Owner's Equity   12,400
Total Liabilities and Owner's Equity $32,400

Appendix 3.2
Debits and Credits

You learned how to use debits and credits to record balance sheet transactions in Appendix 2.2. Let's see if we can use that knowledge to record income statement transactions as well. But first, let's review how debt and credits work with balance sheet accounts. In Figure A3.2.1 we see that debits are used to increase assets and decrease liabilities and equity accounts. Credits, on the other hand, are used to decrease assets and increase liability and equity accounts.

Figure A3.2.1
Debits and Credits

	ASSETS =	LIABILITES + OWNERS' EQUITY
Increase	Debit	Credit
Decrease	Credit	Debit

Recall that temporary accounts (revenues, expenses, gains and losses) are really equity accounts. That means that debits and credits should work the same way with temporary accounts as they do with other equity accounts. Table A3.2.1 below summarizes the effects of temporary accounts on retained earnings (an equity account) and the corresponding use of debits and credits.

To summarize, as shown in Table A3.2.1, an increase in a revenue account increases net income, which increases retained earnings. Credits are used to increase equity accounts like retained earnings, so consequently credits are used to increase revenue accounts. On the other hand, expenses decrease net income, which results in a decrease in retained earnings. Debits are used to decrease equity accounts, like retained earnings, so a debit is used to *increase* expenses accounts and correspondingly *decrease* net income and retained earnings.

Table 3.2.1
Temporary Accounts and Retained Earnings

Temporary Account	Retained Earnings Effect of an Increase in the Temporary Account	Accounting Tool to Increase the Temporary Account
Revenue	Increase	Credit
Expense	Decrease	Debit
Gain	Increase	Credit
Loss	Decrease	Debit

Now we are ready to record the some transactions using debits and credits. Let's use the same transactions as we used in Appendix 3.1:

1. Kids' Klothes sold inventory costing $5,000 for $9.000 in cash,
2. Paid store rent of $1,000,
3. Paid advertising expenses of $400,
4. Paid utilities (electricity, telephone and water) of $300, and
5. Paid interest of $100 on its bank loan.
6. Kids' Klothes also sold a store fixture that cost $800 for $1,000, a $200 gain on the sale.
7. We will ignore taxes in this illustration.

As we record these transactions in journal entry format in Table 3-2.2 remember that every journal entry has five parts:

1. Transaction date, or number in this case,
2. Accounts affected by the transaction,
3. At least one debit,
4. At least one credit, and
5. A description of the transaction.

Table A3.2.2
Transaction Journal Entries

Transaction	Account	Debit	Credit
1	Cash	9,000	
	Revenue		9,000
	Cost of Goods Sold	5,000	
	Inventory		5,000
	To record the sale of inventory costing $5,000 for $9,000 in cash		
2	Rent Expense	1,000	
	Cash		1,000
	To record the payment of one month's rent for $1,000 in cash.		
3	Advertising Expense	400	
	Cash		400
	To record a $400 payment for advertising expense		
4	Utilities Expense	300	
	Cash		300
	To record a $300 payment for utilities expenses.		
5	Interest Expense	100	
	Cash		100
	To record a $100 cash payment for interest on the long-term note payable.		
6	Cash	1,000	
	Store Fixtures		800
	Gain on Sale of Store Fixtures		200
	To record the receipt of cash for the sale of store fixtures that cost $800		

Transaction one includes a new expense account, *cost of goods sold*. This account shows the cost of the goods that were sold to customers. In journal entry one revenue is computed as the number of units sold times the selling price (Revenue = Selling Price (Units Sold)). Cost of goods sold (CGS) is computed as the number of units sold times the cost, rather than the selling price, of the goods (CGS = Cost (Units Sold)).

In journal entry six a debit was used to increase cash (an asset) and credits were used to decrease the asset store fixtures, and to increase the temporary account, gain on sale of store fixtures, which will eventually increase retained earnings.

The final set of journal entries that we need to record are the entries that close the temporary accounts into retained earnings. Most companies use a special account, income summary, in this closing process. Revenue, expense, gain and loss accounts are first closed into income summary. The balance in the income summary account should then equal net income on the income statement. Once the balance in the income summary account is matched to net income on the income statement, proving that all of the temporary accounts have been successfully closed, the income summary account is closed into retained earnings. The closing entries are shown in Table 3-2.3 below. Recall that revenue and gain accounts have normal credit balances, that is, we use credits to increase the account balances. Thus to zero out, or close revenue and gain accounts we debit the corresponding accounts and credit income summary. Expenses and loss accounts have normal debit balances because we use debits to increase the balances of these accounts. Thus to close expense and loss accounts we credit the accounts and debit income summary.

You might want to go back and review how the revenue, gain, and expenses accounts were originally recorded in Table A3.2.2. Then as you review the journal entries below, notice that the opposite sign is used to close the accounts. For example revenue was credited in Table A3.2.2 when sales were originally recorded. Thus revenue is debited in Table A3.2.3 below when the account is closed.

After recording closing journal entries 1 and 2 below, the income summary account has a credit balance of $2,400. That balance is closed into retained earnings in journal entry 3 below.

Table A3.2.2
Closing Journal Entries

Transaction	Account	Debit	Credit
1	Revenue	9,000	
	Gain on Sale of Store Fixtures	200	
	Income Summary		9,200
	To close revenue and gain		
	accounts into income summary.		
2	Income Summary	6,800	
	Cost of Goods Sold		5,000
	Rent Expense		1,000
	Advertising Expense		400
	Utilities Expense		300
	Interest Expense		100
	To close expense accounts into		
	income summary.		
3	Income Summary	2,400	
	Retained Earnings		2,400
	To close income summary into		
	retained earnings.		

To review, after journal entries 1 and 2 above were recorded the balance in the income summary account was $2,400. This resulted from a $9,200 credit to the account in transaction 1 and a $6,800 debit to the account in transaction 2 ($9,200 - $6,800 = $2,400). That balance is equal to net income and was closed to retained earnings in transaction 3. Note as well, that after recording transactions 1 and 2, the balances in the revenue, gain, and expenses accounts were all zero. Thus the two functions of closing entries were met: (1) the balances in the temporary accounts were transferred to income summary, zeroing the temporary accounts, and (2) those balances were then transferred into retained earnings.

Appendix 3.3
Statement of Retained Earnings

You have learned about the balance sheet and the income statement. The third financial statement is the Statement of Retained Earnings. This financial statement acts as a bridge between the income statement and the balance sheet. It shows how last period's retained earnings became the current period's retained earnings. Figure A3.3.1 shows the relationships between the financial statements.

Figure A3.3.1
The Articulation of Financial Statements

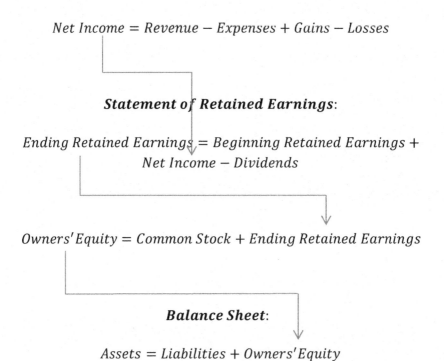

Income Statement:

$$Net\ Income = Revenue - Expenses + Gains - Losses$$

Statement of Retained Earnings:

$$Ending\ Retained\ Earnings = Beginning\ Retained\ Earnings + Net\ Income - Dividends$$

$$Owners'\ Equity = Common\ Stock + Ending\ Retained\ Earnings$$

Balance Sheet:

$$Assets = Liabilities + Owners'\ Equity$$

The statement of retained earnings for Kids' Klothes is simple because the company did not pay any dividends in the month of July. In addition, because it is a new business the balance in the retained earnings account on July 1, the first month of operations, was zero. Figure A3.3.2 shows the Kids' Klothes statement of retained earnings for July.

Figure A3.3.2
Statement of Retained Earnings

Kids' Klothes
Statement of Retained Earnings
For the Month Ended July 31, 2013

Retained Earnings, July 1, 2013	$ -0-
Net Income	2,400
Retained Earnings, July 31, 2013	$2,400

Had Kids' Klothes paid dividends of $1,000 at the end of July then their statement of retained earnings would be as in Figure A3.3.3 below.

Figure A3.3.3
Statement of Retained Earnings (Modified)

Kids' Klothes
Statement of Retained Earnings
For the Month Ended July 31, 2013

Retained Earnings, July 1, 2013	$ -0-
Net Income	2,400
Less Dividends	(1,000)
Retained Earnings, July 31, 2013	$1,400

Chapter 4

Did I Make Any Money? – The Cash Flow Statement

Number one, cash is king... number two,
communicate... number three, buy or bury
the competition.

Jack Welch

The last chapter explained how to measure the profit or loss of a company with the income statement. Profitability is important and companies don't stay in business very long if they don't consistently earn a profit. However, companies can't pay the bills with net income. Bills are paid with cash, something that an accrual-basis income statement doesn't measure.

You said, "Show me the cash!"

Recall that net income is equal to revenue minus expenses. Revenue is recorded when a company:

1. Has sold a good or a service and the earnings process is complete or substantially complete,
2. Can measure the amount of revenue earned, and
3. There is a reasonable probability of payment.

Notice that getting paid is not a requirement for recording revenue. This alone means that there can be a big difference between cash collected from customers and revenue on the income statement. For example if Kids' Klothes sold $100 worth of merchandise to a good customer on July 25 on credit and the customer promised to pay (and did) on August 1 then the $100 of revenue would be recorded in July and included on the income statement when the sale took place, and not in August when the store got paid.

If you are worried about cash flow (the cash flowing into and out of a company) then things get more complicated when we think about expenses. Expenses are reported on the income statement in the period in which they were incurred, not when they are paid. For example, assume that Kids' Klothes received a bill of $250 from the electric company for the month of July on July 28, and the bill was paid on August 1st. That bill represented the cost of electricity used in July. Consequently the $250 utility expenses should be included in the July income statement and not on August's income statement even though the bill was paid in August.

Statement of Cash Flows

The Statement of Cash Flows (also known as the Cash Flow Statement) shows the sources of cash, where cash came from, and the uses of cash. The cash flow statement is divided into three sections, cash flow from operations, cash flow from investing activities, and cash flow from financing activities. The operating activities section of the cash flow statement shows cash received from customers and cash paid for normal business expenses. In short, it shows how much cash the company generated from its business activities.

The investing activities section shows how cash was spent to purchase assets (other than operating assets like inventory). The kinds of assets purchased might include things like investments, property, buildings, and equipment. This section also shows how much cash was received from the sale of these types of assets. Remember in Chapter Three we assumed that Kids' Klothes sold a round for $1,000 and that the sales resulted in a non-operating gain of $200 which was reported on the income statement (selling price $1,000 – cost $800 = gain $200). The $1,000 received from the sale of the round would be reported as a source of cash in the investing activities section of the cash flow statement.

The financing activities section of the cash flow statement shows the sources of cash used to finance the business. Sources of cash used to finance the business include owner investments (the sale of stock for example) and the proceeds from borrowing (bank loans and the sale of bonds). This section also shows the uses of cash for related transactions. If the company financed operations by selling stock then it may decide to pay cash dividends to its stockholders. The payment of cash dividends is a financing activities cash outflow; so are the repayment of loans and the retirement of bonds.

Let's assume that Kids' Klothes completed the following business transactions in July and then we will see what its statement of cash flows looks like.

1. A round (store fixture) costing $800 was sold for $1,000 resulting in a $200 gain.
2. Cash sales were $6,000, and sales on account were $3,000.
3. The cost of the inventory sold was $5,000.
4. A $1,000 check was written for rent.
5. Advertising expenses of $400 were paid in cash.
6. Utility bills for the month of July totaling $300 were received at the end of July and $50 of that was paid before the end of the month.
7. Interest expense of $100 was deduced by the bank in July for interest on the short-term loan.
8. The company computed that it owes $720 in taxes which it will pay at the end of the quarter.
9. Sold 1,000 shares of common stock for $10,000.

Before we look at the Statement of Cash Flows let's review Kids' Klothes' balance sheet and income statement. The balance sheet below as Figure 4.1 shows the account balances on June 30 and July 31. The comparative income statements are shown in Figure 4.2.

Figure 4.1
Kids' Klothes
Balance Sheet
June 30 and July 31, 2013

	June 30	July 31
Assets		
Current Assets		
Cash	$12,000	$27,450
Accounts Receivable	0	3,000
Inventory	10,000	5,000
Total Current Assets	$22,000	$35,450
Property, Plant & Equipment		
Store Fixtures	$ 8,000	$ 7,200
Total Property, Plant & Equipment	8,000	$ 7,200
Total Assets	$30,000	$42,650
Liabilities and Owner's Equity		
Liabilities		
Current Liabilities		
Short-term line of credit	$20,000	$20,000
Utilities expenses payable		250
Income taxes payable		720
Total Liabilities	$20,000	$20,970
Owner's Equity		
Common Stock	$10,000	$20,000
Retained Earnings	0	1,680
Total Owner's Equity	10,000	$21,680
Total Liabilities and Owner's Equity	$30,000	$42,650

Figure 4.2
Kids' Klothes
Income Statement
For the Month Ended July 31, 2013

Revenue	$ 9,000	
Cost of Goods Sold	(5,000)	
Gross Profit		$ 4,000
Operating Expenses		
Rent	($ 1,000)	
Advertising	(400)	
Utilities	(300)	
Total Operating Expenses		(1,700)
Income from Operations		$ 2,300
Other Income & Expenses		
Gain on Sale of Store Fixtures	$ 200	
Interest Expense	(100)	
Total Other Income		100
Income Before Taxes		$ 2,400
Income Tax Expense		(720)
Net Income		$ 1,680

Now that you have reviewed the balance sheets for June and July and the July income statement let's take a look at the July cash flow statement (Figure 4.3).

Figure 4.3

Kids' Klothes
Cash Flow Statement
For the Month Ended July 31, 2013

Cash from operations

Cash collected from customers	$ 6,000
Cash paid for rent	(1,000)
Cash paid for advertising	(400)
Cash paid for utilities	(50)
Cash paid in interest	(100)
Total cash provided by operations	$ 4,450

Cash from investing activities

Cash from the sale of store fixtures	$ 1,000
Total cash provided by investing activities	$ 1,000

Cash from financing activities

Cash provided by the sale of common stock	$10,000

Total cash provided in financing activities	$10,000
Total cash provided	$15,450
Cash balance, June 30, 2013	12,000
Cash balance, July 31, 2013	$27,450

Now it's time to unpack the cash flow statement. By the way, the cash flow statement is the hardest of the financial statements to prepare and probably the hardest to understand, but you will catch on quickly. Let's start at the bottom of the cash flow statement first. The last three lines of Kids' Klothes cash flow statement showed the following:

Total cash provided	$ 15,450
Cash balance, June 30, 2013	12,000
Cash balance, July 31, 2013	$ 27,450

The cash flow statement provides a bridge between one balance sheet and another and shows what caused the prior-period balance sheet to become the current-period balance sheet. It also explains how the cash balance on the June 30, 2013 balance sheet turned into the cash balance on the July 31, 2013 balance sheet. Take a second a compare the cash balance above with the cash balances on the comparative balance sheet in Figure 4.1.

Operating Activities

Recall that an income statement is prepared using accrual accounting. This means that there can be a big difference between the cash that a business generated and its net income. The operating activities section of the cash flow statement provides us with a cash-basis picture of the operations of a business. In essence the operating activities section shows what net income *would have been* had the company used cash-basis accounting rather than accrual accounting.

The operating activities section of the cash flow statement for Kids' Klothes is reproduced below.

Cash from operations	
Cash collected from customers	$ 6,000
Cash paid for rent	(1,000)
Cash paid for advertising	(400)
Cash paid for utilities	(50)
Cash paid in interest	(100)
Total cash provided by operations	$ 4,450

There are two accepted methods for preparing the operating activities section of the cash flow statement. Companies can prepare the statement using either the direct method or the indirect method. Kids' Klothes used the direct method. The direct method shows directly or precisely where operating cash came from and where it went.

When a company prepares a cash flow statement it must choose between using the direct or indirect method to prepare the operating activities section. The direct method is used in this chapter. The direct method is easier for users of financial statements to understand but it is also harder for accountants to prepare. On the other hand, operating activity sections prepared using the indirect method are less intuitive for readers of the financial statements, but are much easier for accountants to prepare.

The indirect method operating activities section is prepared by analyzing the cash-flow effects of changes in non-cash current asset and current liability accounts and applying three simple rules. The rules are:

1. Start with net income from the income statement
2. Reverse the effect of all non-cash items, like gain on sale, that were included on the income statement.
3. Compute the changes in non-cash current assets and current liabilities from one balance sheet to another and:
   a. Add decreases in current assets
   b. Subtract increase in current assets
   c. Subtract decreases in current liabilities
   d. Add increases in current liabilities.

A couple of quick examples will illustrate how intuitive these rules are. Assume that a company made sales of $10,000 on account and that it collected $8,000 of those accounts during the month. Sales on the income statement, and consequently included in net income would be, $10,000. However, only $8,000 was collected from customers. The other $2,000 caused accounts receivable on the balance sheet to increase. If we take revenue from the income statement and use rule 3b from above to subtract the increase in accounts receivable (sales of account during the month that were not collected in cash) we end up with cash collected from customers:

Sales	$10,000
Less increase in accounts receivable	(2,000)
Cash collected from customers	$ 8,000

Let's try that again. Assume that a company had sales, all on account, of $15,000 and that its accounts receivable decreased by $5,000. How much money did it collect from customers? Try to figure it out by using rule 3a above before you look at the box below.

Sales	$15,000
Add decrease in accounts receivable	5,000
Cash collected from customers	$ 20,000

That should make intuitive sense. A decrease in accounts receivable means that the company collected all of the money owed it from current sales, $15,000, plus $5,000 from sales made in previous periods.

Let's take a look at expenses and the corresponding liabilities. Assume that a company reported payroll expenses of $12,000 on its income statement and that wages payable, a current liability that represents wages earned by employees but not yet paid, increased by $4,000. Further assume that net income was $50,000. Let's apply rule 3d from above and see how much cash was used to pay salaries. The rule above says to add the increase in current liabilities to net income.

Net Income	$50,000
Add increase in wages payable	4,000
Cash-basis adjusted net income	$54,000

I hope that makes intuitive sense. If payroll expense was $12,000 but $4,000 of that has not yet been paid then the cash payment for payroll was $8,000 = $12,000 - $4,000. When we convert from accrual net income to cash provided by operations we need to reduce payroll expense to cash paid for wages by $4,000, thus increasing net income by $4,000 (the expense amount that was not paid in cash).

The operating activities section of the cash flow statement for Kids' Klothes when prepared using the indirect method is shown below:

Cash from operations

Net Income	$ 1,680
Adjustments to net income	
Less gain on sales of assets	(200)
Less increase in accounts receivable	(3,000)
Add decrease in inventory	5,000
Add increase in utilities payable	250
Add increase in taxes payable	720
Cash provided by operations	$4,450

The first thing to notice in Kids' Klothes operating activities section is that although cash revenue received from customers is reported, there is no corresponding costs of goods sold or cost of inventory sold even though this item appeared on the income statement. This is because no cash was paid to purchase inventory in July. The inventory was purchased in June and the cash payment for inventory would have appeared on the June cash flow statement. The operating activities section violates the matching principle, that is, it does not match revenue and expenses in the same accounting period. That's alright because the purpose of the cash flow statement isn't to measure income but to show where cash came from and where it went.

Utilities expense on the income statement was $300, but only $50 of related expenses appeared on the cash flow statement. That is because $250 of utility expenses that were incurred in July will be paid in August. The operating activities section only shows the expenses that were paid, not the total of the expenses that were incurred.

Assume that Kids' Klothes had received a $200 utility bill at the end of June and that it was paid, along with $50 of the $300 in July utility bills, in July so that $250 was paid for utilities in July. What do you think utility expenses would be on the June and July income statements, and what would be the cash outflow for utilities be in the operating activities sections of the corresponding cash flow statements for June and July?

Did you come up with an answers? If not, give it a little more thought and then check your answer in the box below.

	June	July
Income Statement		
Utilities Expense	$200	$300
Cash Flow Statement		
Operating Activities		
Cash paid for utilities	$-0-	$250

Well, how did you do? Utility expense should be reported on the income statement in the month that the expenses were incurred. Cash paid for utilities on the cash flow statement, on the other hand, would be reported in the month in which the utility bill was paid.

The other big difference between the income statement and the operating activities section is that a $200 gain on the sale of store fixtures was reported on the income statement but excluded from the operating activities section. Do you remember how the gain was computed? We computed it as:

Cash received from sale of store fixtures	$1,000
Cost of store fixtures sold	(800)
Gain on sale of store fixtures	$ 200

The cash received from the sale, $1,000, is reported in the investing activities section of the cash flow statement. The $200 gain wasn't cash . . . gains are not cash . . . just like net income doesn't represent cash. Consequently the gain was excluded from the cash flow statement and the cash actually received from the sale was included.

Finally you might think that interest paid should be included in the financing activities section of the cash flow statement. This appears logical because the proceeds from taking out a loan would be included in the financing activities section. However, because interest expenses in included on the income statement as a normal business activity, it is also included in the operating activities section. This makes it possible for us to look at the operating activities section as a cash-basis income statement.

Comparative Cash flow Statements

Cash flow statements for both Walmart and Target for the year ended in January 2012 are presented below in Figure 4.4. What can you learn about the two companies by reading their cash flow statements? Take a look and then read on.

Figure 4.4

Walmart and Target
Comparative Cash Flow Statements
For the Year-ended January, 2012
(All Amounts in Thousands)

Period Ending	January 31, 2012	January 27, 2012
Cash flow from Operations		
Net Income	$ 15,699,000	$ 2,929,000
Adjustments for non-cash items		
Depreciation	8,130,000	2,131,000
Adjustments for Changes in Current Assets and Liabilities 637,000		1,117,000
Changes In Accounts Receivables	(796,000)	(187,000)
Changes In Liabilities	2,746,000	353,000
Changes In Inventories	(3,727,000)	(322,000)
Changes In Other Operating Activities	398,000	(107,000)
Total Cash Flow From Operating Activities	$ 24,255,000	$ 5,434,000

Cash flow from Investing Activities

Capital Expenditures	$ (13,510,000)	$ (4,368,000)
Investments	(3,548,000)	151,000
Other Cash flows from Investing Activities	449,000	37,000
Total Cash Flows From Investing Activities	$ (16,609,000)	$ (4,180,000)
Cash flow from Financing Activities		
Dividends Paid	$ (5,048,000)	$ (750,000)
Purchase of Stock	(6,298,000)	(1,753,000)
Net Borrowings	3,130,000	369,000
Other Cash Flows from Financing Activities	(242,000)	(6,000)
Total Cash Flows From Financing Activities	$ (8,458,000)	$ (2,140,000)
Effect Of Exchange Rate Changes	(33,000)	(32,000)
Change In Cash and Cash Equivalents	$ (845,000)	$ (918,000)
Cash and Cash Equivalents, 2011	7,395,000	1,712,000
Cash and Cash Equivalents, 2012	$ 6,550,000	$ 794,000

have noted from the cash flow statements in figure 4.4.

1. Both Walmart and Target used the indirect method to prepare their cash flow statements. You can tell because the first amount on their statements is net income.
2. Walmart generated almost five times as much cash from operations as did Target.
3. Walmart spent about 7.7 times more than Target on inventory purchases.
4. Walmart invested four times as much as did Target.
5. Walmart invested an additional $3.5 billion in securities while Target sold investments to raise cash.
6. Both Walmart and Target used cash to pay dividends and also to purchase their own stock.
7. Walmart raised about eight times as much cash through borrowings as did Target.
8. Although both companies generated significant amounts of cash through operations, both companies spent more cash on investing and financing activities than they took in resulting in reductions in their cash balances of $845 million and $918 million respectively.

Conclusion

An income statement measures the profit earned by a company or the loss that it incurred. It's important and necessary over the long term for a business to earn a profit. However, a business can't deposit profit in the bank and can't write payroll checks or checks to pay suppliers in profit. Ultimately a business needs to generate cash to stay in business. The three sections of the cash flow statement (operating activities, investing activities, and financing activities) provide information about where cash came from and how it was used.

The cash flow statement also acts as a bridge between two balance sheets. By studying a cash flow statement it is possible to understand what caused the changes from last period assets, liabilities and equity to the current period's assets, liabilities and equity.

You have learned about the balance sheet, income statement and cash flow statement. In the next chapter we will learn techniques for analyzing financial statements. Chapter 5 will end our introduction to financial statements. Chapter 6 will explore the ways that accounting choices affect financial statements. An understanding of the effects of accounting choices is required to really understand financial statements, especially if you want to compare the financial statements from different companies.

Chapter 5

Putting it all Together – Financial Statement Analysis

Financial statements tell stories, they tell us what is going on with a company, how well it is doing and where it could improve. Recall in Chapter 1 we compared football and business. The score of a football game will tell you who won but if you want to know more about the game, if didn't have time to watch it or even better play on one of the teams, then you read the game statistics.

I'm serious . . . I'll find out what really happened. Numbers don't lie.

Net income tells us if a company "won", if it earned a profit. If you want to know more about what happened to a company over the course of a year then you read and analyze the annual financial statements. We will focus on three financial statement tools in this chapter, ratio analysis, horizontal (trend) analysis, and vertical (common-sized) analysis. However, before we do that, here is a caution about analysis in general.

Analyze with Caution

Let's assume that for some reason you are interested in the price of an ounce of silver. Maybe you have an ounce of silver that you would like to sell or maybe you would like to buy an ounce of silver. How much would it help you to decide whether to buy or sell silver if I told you that the silver spot price was $23 per ounce today? Not much, in fact, all you would know is that silver is selling today for $23 an ounce. The problem that you would face is that the current spot price, what will we call a price measurement, is a single data point. When we look at a single data point like the price measurement we don't know if that is a good price, if the price is increasing or decreasing, how it compares with the price last year, or how it compares with the expected price in six months. It's hard to make a well-informed decision with a single data point.

We need something against which we can compare our data point, our price measurement, so that we can make well-informed decisions. The three most common sources of comparative data are:

1. Our own subjective expectations,
2. Comparative measurements for the same object at different points in time, and
3. Comparative measurements for different objects at the same point in time.

Let's take a look at each one of these.

Assume again that the current spot price for an ounce of silver is $23 and your informed expectation is that the appropriate price for an ounce of silver is $28 per ounce. Note that this subjective expectation is "an informed" expectation. That means that you know something about silver prices and price movements. Maybe you are a commodities trader with years of experience and you use your experience to create an informed expectation. Given that your informed, subjective expectation is that silver should be selling for $28 an ounce and that the current spot price is $23 per ounce you would probably conclude that silver is underpriced and that this a good time to buy silver but not to sell it.

Rather than basing your analysis on subjective expectations you might gathered time-series data. Time-series data are measurements of an object over time. For example, you might have collected daily spot price data for silver (the measurement object in this case) for the past five days. Your data shows:

Day	Spot Price
1	$25.50
2	$25.35
3	$24.95
4	$24.14
5	$23.45

Given that time-series, and assuming that the past is a good predictor of the future, if the current spot price has decreased from $23.45 on the last day of trading to $23.00 today, what would you expect to happen to the price tomorrow? Like me, you would probably expect the price to decline a little more. Again, a good time to think about buying silver, not such a good time to sell the one ounce of silver that you may own. As an aside, a good way to lose money in the investment markets is to buy when prices are high, and sell when prices are low.

Let's try another time series. What if your five-day time series showed the following:

Day	Spot Price
1	$24.45
2	$23.95
3	$23.15
4	$22.65
5	$22.95

Now what would you think? Compare your current measurement (spot price of $23) to the trend data. It looks to me like the silver market has turned around and I might want to hold on to my one ounce of silver and see how high the price goes before I sell it. Notice how much easier it is to follow trends on a graph than by just looking at a column of numbers.

Finally, we can compare our measurement with other measurements taken at the same time. For example, you might compare Walmart and Target year-end net income percentage, their profit margins, to see which company has done a better job of generating net income. The two companies are not the same but, because they are in the same industry, they are comparable.

Continuing with our example of the silver spot price, what might you use as a comparative external measure? How about the price of gold? You might know, for example, that the prices of the two metals moved together at a fairly constant ratio of 55:1 over the past six months. That means that, on average, an ounce of gold has been selling at price equal to 55 times the price of an ounce of silver or:

(Silver Spot Price) (55) = Gold Spot Price, so
Silver Spot Price = (Gold Spot Price)/55

If the current spot price of gold is $1,100 then our expected spot price for an ounce of silver would be $20, ($20 = $1,100/55). This means that at $23 per ounce silver appears to be overpriced or alternatively that gold appears to be underpriced.

We now know a lot more about the spot price of silver at $23 per ounce than we did before comparing that price to our subjective expectation, to the time-series trend of silver prices, and by comparing the price of silver to the price of gold. Whenever we analyze financial statements we must have something against which we can compare our measurements. We can compare our measurements with our own subjective expectations, time-series trends for the object being measured, or similar measurements from comparable companies.

Ratio Analysis

Ratio analysis makes use of a number of key business ratios as well as other ad hoc ratios that you might develop to analyze a specific company. The key business ratios can be divided into four categories:

1. Short-term solvency ratios,
2. Asset utilization ratios,
3. Leverage ratios, and
4. Profitability ratios.

Short-term Solvency Ratios

Short-term solvency ratios measure a company's ability to meet its current (one year or less) debt obligations. Table 5.1 summarizes the commonly used to short-term solvency ratios.

Table 5.1
Short-term Solvency Ratios

Ratio	Formula	Use
Working Capital *Note: This is a total, and not a ratio*	Current Assets – Current Liabilities	Shows the dollar amount of net current assets or liabilities.
Current Ratio	Current Assets / Current Liabilities	Gives an indication of whether or not the company could meet its current obligations within the current operating cycle.

Ratio	Formula	Use
Quick Ratio	Liquid Current Assets / Current Liabilities Liquid assets include cash, marketable securities, accounts receivable and any other current assets that could instantly be converted into cash.	Shows the dollars of liquid assets available to cover each dollar of current assets.
Current Liabilities to Inventory	Total Current Liabilities / Inventory	Tells how much a firm relies on funds from sale of unsold inventories to meet current debt obligations.
Current Liabilities to Owners' Equity	Total Current Liabilities / Owners' Equity	Contrasts the amounts due to creditors within a year with funds permanently invested by the owners. The smaller the net worth and the larger the liabilities, the greater the risk.

Table 5.2 below shows the calculation of the short-term solvency ratios for Walmart and Target.

Table 5.2
Walmart and Target
2013 Short-term Solvency Ratios
(All dollar amounts are in millions of dollars)

Ratio	Walmart	Target
Working Capital	Current Assets – Current Liabilities $59,940 - $71,818 = ($11,878)	$16,388 - $14,031 = $2,357
Current Ratio	Current Assets / Current Liabilities $59,940 / $71,818 = 83.5%	$16,388 / $14,031 = 116.8%
Quick Ratio	Current Assets – Inventory Current Liabilities ($59,940 - $43,803) / $71,818 = 22.5%	($16,388 – 7,903) / $14,031 = 60.5%
Current Liabilities to Inventory	Total Current Liabilities / Inventory $71,818 / $43,803 = 164.0%	$14,031 / $7,903 = 177.5%
Current Liabilities to Owners' Equity	Total Current Liabilities / Owners' Equity $71,818 / $76,343 = 94.1%	$14,031 / 16,558 = 84.7%

From the first three ratios (working capital, current ratio and quick ratio) we can see that Target has a much stronger current position. That is, Target has a better ability to pay its current obligations using the assets that it has on hand. In fact Target could pay about 60 percent of its current liabilities using its quick assets (primarily cash, cash equivalents and accounts receivable) whereas Walmart could only pay about 20 percent of its obligations. Both companies rely heavily on their ability to turn (sell) inventory to pay their current obligations. Walmart would have to sell 164 percent of its current inventory to pay all of its current liabilities, and Target would have to sell even more, 177.5 percent of its inventory.

Both companies have a fairly high level of short-term leverage risk because their ratios of short-term debt to equity are approaching 100 percent. Walmart's short term debt is about 94 percent of owners' equity. Target has more of a cushion with a lower ratio; short-term debt is about 84 percent of its equity.

Asset Utilization Ratios

Asset utilization ratios provide us with an indication of how well a company is managing and using its assets. Table 5.3 summarizes the most frequently used asset utilization ratios.

Table 5.3
Asset Utilization Ratios

Ratio	*Formula*	*Use*
Accounts Receivable Turnover	Times = Sales / Average Accounts Receivable Average Accounts Receivable = Sales /(Beginning of Period Accounts Receivable + End of Period Accounts Receivable) / 2	Provides an estimate of the number times a company collects all of its accounts receivable over the course of a year.
Average Collection Period	Days = 365 / Accounts Receivable Turnover	Provides an estimate of the number of days it takes a company to collect its receivables.

Ratio	Formula	Use
Inventory Turnover	Times = Cost of Goods Sold / Average Inventory Average Inventory = (Cost of Goods Sold) / (Beginning of Period Inventory + End of Period Inventory) / 2	Provides an estimate of how many times a company sells its inventory over the course of a year.
Average Days in Inventory	Days = 365 / Inventory Turnover	Provides an estimate of how long goods sit in inventory before they are sold.
Estimated Operating Cycle	Days = Average Collection Period + Average Days in Inventory	Provides an estimate of how long it takes to acquire inventory, sell it, accept a receivable, and collect cash from the receivable.
Sales to Working Capital Ratio	Sales / Working Capital	Measures the efficiency of management in using its short-term assets and liabilities to generate sales.
Total Asset Efficiency	Sales / Total Assets	Measures the efficiency of management in using total assets to generate sales.
Ratio of Accounts Payable to Sales	Average Accounts Payable / Sales	Measures the extent to which suppliers' money is being used to generate sales.

Ratio	Formula	Use
Days to Make Payables	Days = 365 x Ratio of Accounts Payable to Sales	This reflects the average number of days it takes a company to pay its suppliers

Now let's take a look at Walmart and Target's asset utilization ratios.

Table 5.4
Walmart and Target
2013 Asset Utilization Ratios
(All dollar amounts are in millions of dollars)

Ratio	Walmart	Target
Accounts Receivable Turnover	Times = Sales / Average Accounts Receivable $\dfrac{\$469,162}{(\$5,937 + \$6,768)/2} = 73.9$ times	$\dfrac{\$73,301}{(\$5,917 + 5,841)/2} = 12.5$ times
Average Collection Period	Days = 365 / Accounts Receivable Turnover 365 / 73.9 times = 4.9 days	365 / 12.5 times = 29.3 days
Inventory Turnover	Times = Cost of Goods Sold / Average Inventory $\dfrac{\$352,488}{(\$40,714 + 43,803)/2} = 8.3$ times	$\dfrac{\$50,568}{(\$7,918 + 7,903)/2} = 6.4$ times

Ratio	Walmart	Target
Average Days in Inventory	Days = 365 / Inventory Turnover 365 / 8.3 times = 43.8 days	365 / 6.4 times = 57.1 days
Estimated Operating Cycle	Days = Average Collection Period + Average Days in Inventory 4.9 days + 43.8 days = 48.7 days	29.3 days + 57.1 days = 86.4 days
Sales to Working Capital Ratio	Sales / Working Capital $469,162 / ($11,878) = -39.5	$73,301 / 2,357 = 31.1
Total Asset Efficiency	Sales / Total Assets $469,162 / $203,105 = 231.0%	$73,301 / $48,163 = 152.2%
Ratio of Accounts Payable to Sales	Average Accounts Payable / Sales $\frac{(55,952 + 59,099)/2}{\$469,162} = 12.3\%$	$\frac{(10,501 + 11,037)/2}{\$73,301} = 14.7\%$

Ratio	Walmart	Target
Days to Make Payables	Days = 365 x Ratio of Accounts Payable to Sales 365 x .123 = 44.8 days	365 x .147 = 53.6 days

Let's look at accounts receivable management first. Why do you think that Walmart apparently does a better job of collecting its accounts receivable than does Target? After all, it appears that Walmart collects its customer accounts in just 5 days whereas Target takes 29.3 days. Here is where knowing about the companies you are analyzing becomes important. Both Walmart and Target accept credit and debit cards and it takes a few days for payments on debit and credit cards to be processed and the amount collected from the credit card company to be deposited in Walmart and Target's accounts. However, that doesn't explain the difference. Walmart doesn't have a company-branded credit card, Target does.

When wee computed the accounts receivable turnover we used total sales in the numerator. Had we used credit sales the numerator would have been smaller and the number of turns (the number of times all of the accounts receivable are collected in a year) would have been lower, resulting in a higher average collection period. For example, let's assume that 20 percent of Target's sales are made to customers who use the Target store-branded credit card. In that case the accounts receivable turnover would have been computed as:

$$Accounts\ Receivable\ Turnover = \frac{\$73,301\ x\ 0.20}{\frac{\$5,917 + \$5,841}{2}} = \frac{\$14,440}{\$5,879}$$

$$= 2.46\ times$$

and the average collection period would be:

$$Average\ Collection\ Period = \frac{365}{2.46} = 148.6\ days$$

It appears that Walmart does a better job than Target of managing its inventory. Goods sitting in a warehouse, in transit to a store, in a stock room, or on the shelves tie up resources and they are unproductive until sold. It costs money to buy inventory and store it, and inventory doesn't generate sales or cash until it is sold. On average Walmart turns over its entire inventory 8.3 times a year and it holds inventory for 43.8 days before sale. Obviously some items sell faster, like lettuce in the produce section, and other lower-demand items sell more slowly, but on average Walmart takes 43.8 days to sell its inventory.

Target on the other hand only turns its inventory over 6.4 times a year and that means that on average goods are in inventory for 57.1 days before they are sold. If you were a product-line manager at Target would probably be looking at what you could do to move inventory faster. If you owned a small business you would monitor your inventory levels, identify slow-moving items and decide what to do to move them out the door; and then decide if those slow-moving items really belong in your store at all.

Operating Cycle – The operating cycle is the time that it takes to use cash to buy inventory, sell the inventory and create an account receivable, collect the account receivable and finally have cash again. The operating cycle is depicted in Figure 5.2 below.

114

Figure 5.2
Operating Cycle

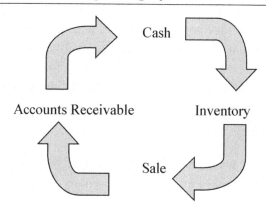

It appears from our analysis that Walmart's operating cycle, 48.7 days, is substantially less than Target's 86.4 days. Most of this is due to the longer time that it takes Target to convert accounts receivables into cash. Even so, Target's number of days in inventory is almost two weeks long than that of Walmart.

Leverage Ratios

Leverage, defined simply, is using other people money to make money. Financial managers try to balance the amount of debt (loans) and capital (owner investments) to maximize firm performance without increasing risk to an unacceptably high level. Debt causes risk . . . the risk that a company will not be able to meet it debt obligations.

Leverage, and why it is used, can be a difficult concept so let's use a simple example to show how leverage works. Assume that Anne and Bill are good friends and have decided to purchase homes in the same neighborhood. After looking at lots of new developments they pick two identical homes next door to each other. Both houses cost $200,000. Anne has never liked debt so she saved money for years so that she could buy her home outright. At closing she wrote a check for $200,000 and took possession of her new home. Bill, on the other hand, thinks that using other people's money is a good idea so he paid 10 percent down ($20,000) at closing and took out a 15-year mortgage for the $180,000 balance of the purchase price. A year later Anne and Bill decide to get married and they both sell their homes for $220,000 and then purchase a new home together in a different development. See, they story had a happy ending.

Anne and Bill both realized $20,000 gains on the sales of their original homes:

Selling Price $220,000

Original Cost   (200,000)

Gain on Sale $ 20,000

However, their investments were different. Anne invested $200,000 in her home so her return on her investment was 10 percent:

$$Return\ on\ Investment = ROI = \frac{Gain}{Investment}$$

$$Anne'sReturn\ on\ Investment = \frac{\$20,000}{\$200,000} = 0.10 = 10\ percent$$

Bill, on the other hand only invested $20,000 (we will ignore the small amount of additional investment from his monthly mortgage payments because most of the initial monthly mortgage payments went to interest on the loan) so his return on investment is:

$$Return\ on\ Investment = ROI = \frac{Gain}{Investment}$$

$$Bill'sReturn\ on\ Investment = \frac{\$20,000}{\$20,000} = 1.00 = 100\ percent$$

Bill had a higher return on his investment because, although the dollar gains on sale were the same, he had invested less. Note that if the homes were sold of a loss rather than a gain Bill's loss on investment would also have been higher than Anne's . . . high leverage increases risk. If the market took a down turn and Anne and Bill each sold their homes for $175,000, a $25,000 loss then their ROIs would be:

$$Anne'sReturn\ on\ Investment = \frac{\$25,000}{\$200,000} = -0.125 = -12.5\ percent$$

$$Bill'sReturn\ on\ Investment = \frac{\$-25,000}{\$20,000} = -1.25 = -125\ percent$$

As you can see, leverage increases ROI going both directions. To receive a higher return, a higher ROI in this case, you also bear the risk of higher down-side risk.

Now, assume that you are thinking about investing in one of two companies. Both companies earned net income of $1 million last year and both companies had total assets of $20 million.. Company One had total debt of $10 million. So, using the accounting equation you know that Company One must have owner's equity of $10 million. Company Two is more highly leveraged. It has total liabilities of $15 million so its owners' equity must total $5 million. As a potential investor you are interested in the return on equity (ROE) of these two potential investments. For now you might think of ROE as the percentage return (interest earned) on the investment that owners have made in the company. It is computed as:

$$ROE = \frac{NetIncome}{Owners'Equity}$$

ROE for Company One is 10% (Net Income $1 million / Owners' Equity $10 million) and ROE for Company Two is 20% (Net Income $1 million / Owners' Equity $5 million). Is Company Two a better investment because it has a higher ROE? Don't know . . . it depends on how much risk you are willing to take. Leverage ratios measure risk, risk related to using debt to finance operations.

Common leverage ratios are summarized in Table 5.5 below.

Table 5.5
Leverage Ratios

Ratio	Formula	Use
Times Interest Earned	Net Income before Interest and Taxes / Interest Expense	Used to measure the ability of a company to meet its interest payment obligations. Note that failure to make interest payments may result in technical default on loans which may lead to bankruptcy.
Debt to Equity Ratio	Total Debt / Total Equity	Indicates the extent to which debt financing is used to fund operations.
Debt to Total Assets	Total Debt / Total Assets	Indicates the extent to which debt financing is used to fund asset acquisition.

Now let's take a look at Walmart and Target again and see how they use leverage. As depicted in Table 5.6 below both Walmart and Target easily earn enough to cover interest expenses and so neither company is in danger of missing interest payments. Target is more highly leveraged than Walmart with debt amounting to 190 percent to equity and by funding about 66 percent of their assets with debt. We will see the effect of leverage on profitability ratios in the next section.

Table 5.6
Walmart and Target Leverage Ratios
(All dollar amounts are in millions of dollars)

Ratio	Walmart	Target
Times Interest Earned	Net Income before Interest and Taxes (Net Income + Interest Expense + Taxes) /Interest Expense $\dfrac{\$16,999 + \$2,251 + \$7,981}{\$2,251} = 12.1$	NOTE: The answer, 7.0, is in number of time. $\dfrac{\$2,000 + \$762 + \$1,610}{\$762} = 7.0$
Debt to Equity Ratio	Total Debt / Total Equity $126,243 / \$76,343 = 1.7 =$ 170%	$31,605 / \$16,558 = 1.9 =$ 190%
Debt to Total Assets	Total Debt / Total Assets $126,243 / \$203,105 = .622 =$ 62.2%	$31,605 / \$48,163 = .656 =$ 65.6%

Profitability Ratios

Profitability ratios provide us with different ways to measure a company's financial performance. Net income is the primary profitability measure and is the basis for many of the ratios with give us different ways to measure performance.

Table 5.7
Profitability Ratios

Ratio	Formula	Use
Earnings per Share (Basic)	(Net Income – Preferred Dividends) / WACSO WACSO = Weighted Average Common Shares Outstanding	Provides a measure of net income attributable to or earned by every share of common stock.
Profit Margin	Net Income / Sales	Indicates the percentage of every sales dollar that remains as net income after all business expenses.
Return on Assets	Net Income / Total Assets	Indicates the percentage return on every dollar invested in assets.
Return on Equity	Net Income / Total Equity	Indicates the percentage return on every dollar invested by stockholders as direct investment or retained earnings. Note that retained earnings represents the amount earned over time by a corporation that *was not* paid to stockholders as dividends.

Once again it's time to turn to our comparison of Walmart and Target. We know that Walmart is considerably bigger than Target and that as a result they have a much higher net income figure, about $17 billion compared to about $3 billion. However, using key profitability ratios we might be able to learn a little more.

As you can see in Table 5.8, Walmart was more profitable that Target on a per-share basis. That means that Walmart generates more net income per share of common stock (weighted-average number of common shares outstanding) than does Target.

Table 5.8
Walmart and Target Profitability Ratios
(All dollar amounts are in millions of dollars)

Ratio	Walmart	Target
Earnings per Share (Basic)[2]	(Net Income – Preferred Dividends) / WACSO $5.02 / share	$4.52
Profit Margin	Net Income / Sales $16,999 / $469,162 = 3.6%	$2,999 / $73,301 = 4.1%
Return on Assets	Net Income / Total Assets $16,999 / $203,105 = 8.4%	$2,999 / $48,163 = 6.2%
Return on Equity	Net Income / Total Equity $16,999 / $76,343 = 22.3%	$2,999 / $16,558 = 18.1%

Target on the other hand does a better job of converting sales dollars into net income. Walmart turns 3.6 cents out of every sales dollar into profit while

---

[2] The earnings per share calculations are complex and beyond the scope of this book. The formula given in tables 5.7 and 5.8 works for the simplest case where a firm has a very simple capital structure. The EPS numbers given in Table 5.8 were taken from Yahoo finance.

Target converts 4.1 cents of every sales dollar into net income. There are several ways that Target could be doing this. They might be selling their products with a higher mark-up on cost, have lower cost of goods sold, or do a better job of controlling expenses. We will learn more to help us answer this question when we look at vertical analysis below.

Walmart is more profitable than Target when we look at return on assets and return on equity as well (8.4% and 22.3% to Targets' 6.2% and 18.1%). DuPont analysis can help us better understand what drives these differences.

DuPont Analysis

The DuPont Company is responsible for the development of many of the key business ratios that we use, and the relationship between them. You know that Return on Assets (ROA) is computed by dividing net income by total assets. However, DuPont analysis provides us with a more complete picture of how assets are being used. It recognizes that there is an important relationship between ratios, between ROA, profit margin and total asset efficiency:

$$ROA = Total\ Asset\ Efficiency\ x\ Profit\ Margin$$

$$ROA = \frac{Sales}{Total\ Assets}\ x\ \frac{Net\ Income}{Sales} = \frac{Net\ Income}{Total\ Assets}$$

Notice that ROA is really all about how well a company uses its assets to generate sales (total asset efficiency ratio) and then how well the company is able to control costs so that sales turn into net income (profit margin).

The same kind of relationships hold with return on equity (ROE). You know that ROE is net income divided by owners' equity:

$$ROE = \frac{Net\ Income}{Owners'Equity}$$

As with ROA, ROE is really the function of related ratios. One way to look at ROE is as:

$$ROE = ROA \; x \; Asset \; to \; Equity \; Ratio$$

and,

$$ROE = \frac{Net \; Income}{Total \; Assets} \; x \; \frac{Total \; Assets}{Owners' Equity} = \frac{Net \; Income}{Owners' Equity}$$

and,

$$ROE = \frac{Sales}{Total \; Assets} \; x \; \frac{Net \; Income}{Sales} \; x \; \frac{Total \; Assets}{Owners' Equity}$$

which means that:

$$ROE$$
$$= Asset \; Efficiency \; Ratio \; x \; Profit \; Margin \; x \; Asset \; to \; Equity \; Ratio$$

This tells us that owner financing leads to asset acquisition. Acquired assets result in sales and that cost control (the ability to turn sales dollars into net income) results in net income.

Let's return to our comparative analysis of Walmart and Target and see what we can learn from their ROA and ROE calculations seen through the lens of DuPont analysis.

When we recomputed return on assets for both Walmart and Target using the DuPont formulations we see the following:

$$ROA = Profit \; Margin \; x \; Total \; Asset \; Efficiency$$

$$ROA_{Walmart} = \frac{\$16,999}{\$469,162} \; x \; \frac{\$469,162}{\$203,105} = .036 \; x \; 2.31 = .084 = 8.4\%$$

$$ROA_{Target} = \frac{\$2,999}{\$73,301} \; x \; \frac{\$73,301}{\$48,163} = .041 \; x \; 1.52 = .062 = 6.2\%$$

Using the DuPont analysis we can better understand why Walmart's ROA was greater than Target's. Walmart had a significantly higher asset efficiency ratio than did Target. Walmart was better at using its assets to generate sales.

Recall that the easy way to compute ROE is by using the formula:

$$ROE = \frac{Net\ Income}{Owners'\ Equity}$$

but once again, we can gain better insight if we use the DuPont analysis approach:

$$ROE = \frac{Sales}{Total\ Assets} \ x \ \frac{Net\ Income}{Sales} \ x \ \frac{Total\ Assets}{Owners'\ Equity}$$

$$ROE_{Walmart} = \frac{\$469,162}{\$203,105} \ x \ \frac{\$16,999}{\$469,162} \ x \ \frac{\$203,105}{\$76,343} = 2.31 \ x \ .036 \ x \ 2.66$$
$$= .223 = 22.3\%$$

$$ROE_{Target} = \frac{\$73,301}{\$48,163} \ x \ \frac{\$2,999}{\$73,301} \ x \ \frac{\$48,163}{\$16,558} = 1.52 \ x \ .041 \ x \ 2.91$$
$$= .181 = 18.1\%$$

Once again, although Target has better (higher) profit margin and asset to equity ratios Walmart's higher asset efficient ratio made the difference between the two companies' return on equity.

Horizontal Analysis

Horizontal analysis is sometimes called trend analysis. Horizontal analysis is used to determine how financial statement components have changed over time. For example, horizontal analysis might tell us that sales have increased 15 percent over the past year. Horizontal analysis can be used a number of different ways. First, it can simply be used to measure growth rates. Second, it can be used to determine if the growth rates for related financial statement accounts are similar, and third, it can be used to compare growth rates across companies.

In the example above, if we know that sales increased 15 percent over the previous year then we might logically expect that cost of goods sold would also have increased about 15 percent, and maybe even that accounts receivable would have increased by about the same amount. This is an example of using horizontal analysis to study the changes in related accounts. Changes in the growth rates for related accounts that depart from our expectations should cause us to ask "why?" questions. For example, if sales increased by 15 percent but cost of goods sold increased by 20 percent, what happened? Did the company experience an increase in inventory cost that wasn't passed on to customers? Or, was there an interruption in the supply chain that caused a shortage resulting in increased factor prices? We don't know, but horizontal analysis can direct our attention and lead us to dig deeper.

Below we will look at the third use of horizontal analysis when we compare selected accounts for Walmart and Target. But first, let's discover how to do horizontal analysis. There are two alternatives, and you should be familiar with both, because you will encounter both in your career. The two approaches are period-to-period changes, and changes from a base period. The period-to-period percentage change in an account is computed as:

$$Period - to - Period\ Percentage\ Change$$
$$= \frac{Current\ Period\ Balance - Prior\ Period\ Balance}{Prior\ Period\ Balance}$$

Note that in this formula a period could be a month, a quarter, a year, or any other period of time that is relevant for analysis and decision making. Let's assume that Kids' Klothes sales last month were $14,000 and this month sales increased to $18,000. What is the period-to-period or month-to-month sales growth? Let's use our formula:

$$Period - to - Period\ Percentage\ Change = \frac{\$18,000 - \$14,000}{\$14,000}$$
$$= .286 = 28.6\%$$

So now we know that sales increased 28.6 percent from one month to another. What would you do with that information? If I owned Kid's

Klothes I would want to know what caused the sales increase, and what I could do to keep increasing sales.

Change from a base period is computed almost the same way. The formula is:

Percentage Change from a Base Period

$$= \frac{Current\ Period\ Balance - Base\ Period\ Balance}{Base\ Period\ Balance}$$

To compute changes from a base period it is necessary to select a base period. Many companies use the same base period year after year. If, for example a company selected year-end balances in 1995 as their base year then all changes would be computed from that year. Let's assume that Kids' Klothes has selected July 31, 2013 as its base period and compare the growth rates computed using the period-to-period and base period calculations.

Table 5.9
Kids' Klothes
Horizontal Analysis of Sales
Monthly for the Period from July 31, 2013 to December 31, 2013

Month	Sales	Period-to-Period Percent Change	Change from the Base Period (July 31, 2013)
July	$14,000		
August	$18,000	28.6%	28.6%
September	$20,000	11.1%	42.9%
October	$18,000	-10.0%	28.6%
November	$16,000	-11.1%	14.3%
December	$22,000	37.5%	57.1%

First note that there are no growth rates for July, this is because there was no preceding month from which the change could be computed. The period-to-period change for October was computed as ($18,000 - $20,000) / $20,000 =

-$2,000 / $20,000 = -10.0%. The base period percent change for the same month was computed as ($18,000 - $14,000) / $14,000 = $4,000 / $14,000 = 28.6%. Which is more informative? Well, it depends. As a manager or owner is it more useful to know that sales decreased 10 percent from September to October, or that sales in October were 28.6 percent higher than they were in July? Period-to-period analysis gives you a short-term snapshot of what happened while the percent change from a base period gives you a longer-term picture.

Remember that we can also use horizontal analysis to learn about two different companies. Let's take a look now at Walmart and Target. While you could perform horizontal analysis of every financial statement line item, let's just take a look at sales, cost of goods sold and inventory for the two companies.

Table 5.10
Walmart and Target
Horizontal Analysis of Selected Accounts
For the Years Ended 2013 and 2012
(All Amounts are in Billions of Dollars)

Account	Walmart 2013	Walmart 2012	% Chng	Target 2013	Target 2012	% Chng
Sales	$469,162	$446,950	4.97%	$73,301	$69,865	4.92%
Cost of Sales	$352,448	$335,127	5.17%	$50,568	$47,860	5.66%
Inventory	$43,803	$40,714	7.59%	$7,903	$7,918	- 0.19%
Net Income	$16,999	$15,699	8.28%	$2,999	$2,929	2.39%

Horizontal analysis shows us that both Walmart's and Target's sales grew at almost 5 percent from 2012 to 2013. Walmart's year end in 2013 was January 31, 2013 while Target's was February 1, 2013 so their financial statements covered about the same period of time. Cost of sales for both companies increased faster than did their sales growth so we might assume that they didn't pass along all of the cost increases to customers through higher prices. Walmart's inventory increased faster than did its sales from 2012 to 2013 while Target's inventory declined but was essentially the same in 2013 as it was in 2012. Finally Walmart showed an 8.28 percent increase in net income in 2013 over 2012. This grow rate was almost twice the growth rate in sales so we might look at other expenses to see where they controlled their costs. Target, on the other hand, grew its net income at a rate that was about half of the growth rate in sales. Thus we might question where they incurred higher expenses. Vertical analysis might help us better understand what happened to Target in 2013.

Vertical Analysis

In vertical analysis, also known as common sized financial statements, we convert all of the dollar amounts on a financial statement to percentages. This helps us better understand the composition or financial structure of the business and it can also help us compare the structure of companies that have very different sizes, like Walmart and Target.

We express all of the numbers on a financial statement as a percentage of a key number to prepare common-sized financial statements. All of the dollar amounts on an income statement are expressed as a percentage of net sales (or sales if a company doesn't report net sales, which are sales less sales discounts and sales returns and allowances). All of the dollar amounts on a balance sheet are expressed as a percentage of total assets. Thus cash would be shows as a percentage of total assets, and so would accounts payable and common stock.

Table 5.11 on the next page presents condensed income statements for both Walmart and Target for the years ended 2012. Notice how hard it is to analyze the differences between the two companies when the financial statements are presented in dollars.

Table 5.11
Walmart and Target
Comparative Income Statements
For the Year-ended January, 2012
(All Amounts in Millions)

	Walmart	Target
Total Revenue	$446,950	$69,865
Less Cost of Goods Sold	335,127	47,860
Gross Profit	$111,823	$22,005
Less Operating Expenses		
Selling, General & Administrative	85,265	14,552
Other		2,131
Income from Operations	$ 26,558	$ 5,322

Now let's show the same financial statement as common-sized financial statements where all amounts are shown as a percentage of sales.

Table 5.12
Walmart and Target
Comparative Common-Sized Income Statements
For the Year-ended January, 2012
(All Amounts in Millions)

	Walmart	Target
Total Revenue	100.0%	100.0%
Less Cost of Goods Sold	75.0	68.5
Gross Profit	25.0	31.5
Less Operating Expenses		
Selling, General & Administrative	19.1	20.8
Other		3.1
Income from Operations	5.9%	7.6%

Walmart and Target's income statements are much easier to compare after they have been converted to common-sized financial statements. Now we can see that Walmart spend about 75 cents of every sales dollar to cover the cost of the goods sold while Target only spend 68.5 cents out of every sales dollar to cover to the cost of inventory sold. There are two ways that this could happen. First, Walmart might spend more to purchase inventory than does Target. Or, it could be that Walmart doesn't use as high of a markup on cost when its sets sales prices. Which do you think is the more likely explanation? Walmart did a better job of controlling operating costs than did Target, but that difference wasn't enough to overcome the cost of goods sold differential. Walmart only had 25 cents left from every sales dollar to cover operating expenses and provide a profit (5.9 cents out of every sales dollar) while Target had 31.5 cents left out of every sales dollar to cover operating expenses and provide a profit of 7.6 cents out of every sales dollar.

Table 5.13 below presents a partial balance sheet (assets only) for Walmart as of their fiscal year end in 2012 and 2011. The amounts shown are in dollars and also common sized (percent of total assets). Notice how much easier year-to-year comparison is when the amounts are common sized.

Table 5.13
Walmart
Partial Balance Sheet
(Dollar Amounts and Percentages)
January 31, 2012 and 2011

	2012	2011	2012	2011
Current Assets				
Cash	$ 6,550	$ 7,395	3.4%	4.1%
Accounts receivable, net	5,937	5,089	3.1%	2.8%
Inventories	40,714	36,437	21.1%	20.2%
Prepaid expenses	1,685	2,960	0.9%	1.6%
Assets of discontinued operations	89	131	0.0%	0.1%
Total current assets	$ 54,975	$ 52,012	28.4%	28.8%
Property, plant & equipment, net	109,603	105,098	56.7%	58.1%
Leased assets, net	2,721	2,780	1.4%	1.5%
Goodwill & other intangible assets	26,107	20,892	13.5%	11.6%
Total assets	$ 193,406	$ 180,782	100.0%	100.0%

For most companies, including Walmart, the composition of the financial statements don't change very much from year-to-year. You can see above that there was some reallocation of current assets from one account to another from 2011 to 2012. For example cash, in dollar amount and as a percentage of total assets, decreased from 2011 to 2012 while inventories increased slightly. Nevertheless that amount of current assets, as a percentage of total assets, changed only slightly from 2011 to 2012.

Large, unexpected, and unexplained changes in financial statement structure are usually red flags that indicate that something unusual has happened.

Financial Statement Fraud

Remember the dictum at the beginning of this chapter, the one that stated that numbers don't lie. Numbers don't lie, but sometimes people do and they try to use numbers to hide the truth. Accountants talk about errors and irregularities in accounting records and financial statements. Errors are unintentional mistakes. They are just problems that need to be corrected. Irregularities are something else. When an auditor states that there are irregularities in a financial statement the auditor is really saying that it appears that fraud has occurred.

A legal definition of fraud is that it is a false representation of a material fact or the concealment of what should have been disclosed that is intended to deceive another so that the individual will act or not act upon the false representation to his or her legal injury. When we talk about financial statement fraud we mean the intentional misrepresentation of material disclosures in the financial statements done to deceive users of the financial statements so that they would engage in actions, that they would otherwise not have taken, and do so to their economic harm.

For example, a company might overstate net income be recording fraudulent sales and conceal those fraudulent sales by recording fictitious accounts receivable. Thus both the income statement and balance sheet would be misstated. However, a banker, seeing sales growth and an increase in net income might grant a loan that might not otherwise have been given, and one with the company receiving the loan will never be able to repay. Potential investors might see the increase in net income and decide that the company is

132

a good investment, and buy stock in the company for a price far above its real worth.

Does fraudulent financial reporting really happen? Of course it does, and it has a long history. Back in 1982 the New York Times reported that,

> "Saxon, a paper products and business machines concern based in New York, had reported profits in each of the first three quarters of 1981. Suddenly, it announced an estimated loss of $47 million for all of 1981, filed for bankruptcy, and made a series of disclosures of false financial reports that have brought it into a storm of controversy.
>
> "Saxon's real financial condition has become shrouded in mystery. On June 21, the company said the value of inventory in its business products division had been overstated by about $24 million. A week later, it said the overstatement may "substantially exceed" $24 million."[3]

It turned out the Saxon had been engaged in a 14-year, inventory overstatement fraud. Over the course of the fraud they created so much fictitious inventory that they had to create a fictitious warehouse in which to "store" the inventory.

Figure 5.14 below summarizes ten of the worst recent financial statement frauds.

---

[3] Lueck, T. J.. (1982). Sorting out the Saxon Tangle. The New York Times (15 June). Retrieved from http://www.nytimes.com/1982/07/15/ business/ sorting-out-the-saxon-tangle.html

Figure 5.14
Worst Financial Statement Frauds

Company/Year	Estimated Loss	Misstatement
Waste Management 1998	$1.7 billion in fake earnings	Understated depreciation expense and accumulated depreciation
ENRON 2001	$74 billion in shareholders losses	Kept huge debts off the balance sheet
Worldcom 2002	$11 billion in inflated assets	Fictitious revenue and understated expenses
TYOC 2002	CEO and CFO stole $150 million Overstated net income by $500 million	Unapproved loans, fraudulent stock sales, theft disguised as executive bonuses and benefits
HealthSouth 2003	$1.4 billion in inflated net income	Management instructed accountants to make up numbers and transactions from 1996 – 2003.
Freddie Mac 2003	$5 billion in inflated net income	Intentional misstatement of earnings
American Insurance Group 2005	$3.9 billion including rigged bids and stock price manipulation	Recorded loan proceeds as revenue, directed clients to insurance companies with whom AIG had payoff agreements, told traders to inflate stock prices
Lehman Brothers 2008	$50 billion is fraudulent sales	Disguised $50 billion in loans as sales of toxic assets to Cayman Island banks with the understanding that the assets would be repurchased by Lehman. Overstated cash by $50 billion and understated toxic assets by the same amount.
Bernie Madoff 2008	$64.8 billion in investor losses	Ponzi scheme
Saytam 2009	$1.5 billion in overstated revenue	Falsified revenue, margins and cash balances

According to the Association of Certified Fraud Examiners asset misappropriation (the theft of assets) is the most common type of occupation fraud and abuse. It accounted for about 85 percent of the reported frauds in 2014. However, the loss per incident was "only" $130,000. This pales in comparison to the average loss of $1,000,000 per incident of fraudulent financial reporting (9 percent of occupation fraud and abuse cases).[4]

Discovering Financial Statement Fraud

Probably the best first rule for uncovering fraud in financial statements is that if it looks too good to be true it probably *is* too good to be true. Take, for example, the case of MiniScribe, a 1980s hard drive manufacturer. The company reported a loss of $16,777,000 on its 1985 year-end income statement. In one of the best turnarounds in history that loss, one year later, had turned into positive net income of $22,725,000, a change of $39,502,000 in just one year.

By digging just a little bit further into the financial statements we can learn much more. Figure 5.15 shows selected income statement and balance sheet information for MiniScribe.

Figure 5.15
MiniScribe
Selected Financial Information

	1986	*1985*
Sales	$184,861	$113,951
Cost of Goods Sold	$137,936	$111,445
Gross Profit	$ 46,925	$ 2,506
Net Income	$ 22,725	($16,769)
Accounts Receivable	$ 40,518	$ 16,777
Inventory	$ 45,106	$ 22,501
Total Assets	$136,877	$ 81,866

The rule of thumb in searching for red flags (warning indicators) on financial statements is to look for unusual changes and relationships. Figures 5.16 and

[4] Association of Certified Fraud Examiners. (2014). *Report to the Nations on Occupational Fraud and Abuse: 2014 Global Fraud Study*. Retrieved from http://www.acfe.com/rttn/docs/2014-report-to-nations.pdf

5.17 below show trend and common sized analyzes of the selected financial information found in Figure 5.15. Take a good look at the two tables that follow and see if you can identify any red flags.

Table 5.16
MiniScribe
Trend Analysis of Selected Financial Information

	1985-1986 % Change
Sales	62.2%
Cost of Goods Sold	23.8%
Gross Profit	1772.5%
Net Income	235.5%
Accounts Receivable	141.5%
Inventory	100.5%
Total Assets	67.2%

Table 5.17
MiniScribe
Common-size Analysis of Selected Financial Information

	1986	1985
Sales	100%	100%
Cost of Goods Sold	75%	98%
Gross Profit	25%	2%
Net Income	12%	-15%
Accounts Receivable	30%	20%
Inventory	33%	27%
Total Assets	100%	100%

So, did you discover any red flags? Table 5.18 includes some of the red flags that you should have detected. These are red flags that, had you been a securities analyst in 1986, would have caused to you dig deeper, to suspect that something was rotten in MiniScribe, and that should have made you very cautious about recommending or holding stock in MiniScribe.

Table 5.18
MiniScribe
Financial Statement Red Flags

1. Sales increased 62.2 percent from 1985 to 1986. Cost of goods sold and gross profit should have increased at about the same rate. However, cost of goods sold only increased 23.8 percent while gross profit increased a whopping 1,772.5 percent. This is an indicator of fraudulent sales; sales that were recorded without an accompanying cost of goods sold.

2. Accounts receivable and inventory increased much faster than did sales, 141.5 percent and 100.5 percent respectively. I would expect them both to grow at about the same rate as sales.

3. In 1985 cost of goods sold was 98 percent of sales. That declined to 75 percent of sales in 1986. That's marvelous cost control, or could it be fraud?

4. The reduction of cost of goods sold, as a percentage of sales, resulted in a startling increase in gross profit; from 2 percent of sales in 1985 to 25 percent of sales in 1986.

5. Net income, as a percentage of sales, grew from -15 percent to +12 percent.

6. Both accounts receivable and inventory grew as a percentage of total assets.

So what happened at MiniScribe? They were competing with other hard drive manufacturers for a big contract to supply IBM with hard drives for their new personal computer. To demonstrate that they had the capacity to meet IBM's requirements MiniScribe built a new factory, and then they lost the bid. That led to cash flow problems. Late in 1986 MiniScribe started packaging bricks, yes, real bricks, as hard drives and then shipping them to a customer in the Far East. Their plan was to contact the customer at the beginning of the next year and to request the return of "defective" hard drives (bricks) identified by specific serial numbers on the boxes. This resulted in a big increase in sales without a corresponding increase in cost of goods sold. The practice was leaked to the press and MiniScribe quickly declared bankruptcy.

The most common objective of fraudulent financial reporting is to increase net income. That usually results in a corresponding increase in accounts receivable as well. Increasing revenue can be done several ways, the two most common ways are to (1) record fictitious sales, and (2) to record sales early. You can often detect both practices by looking for an increase in sales and accounts receivable without a corresponding increase in cost of goods sold.

The second approach to overstating revenue is particularly dangerous for a company. Assume that a company is getting close to the end of the first quarter and knows that it will not meet analyst expectations. The executive team decides to record orders that will be filled early in the second quarter as first quarter sales, thus boosting sales and helping the division meet its targets. They just violated revenue recognition rules and created a new problem. Now that sales for the second quarter sales have been misappropriated and moved to the first quarter, second quarter sales are likely to be below target . . . this leads to a need to "borrow" even more sales from the third quarter. The pattern continues, quarter-to-quarter, until year end when sales have to be "borrowed" from the next year, and the fraud now has to be hidden from the auditors. What may have started out as a little bit of window dressing has become a major fraud.

The Sarbanes-Oxley Act

The Sarbanes-Oxley Act of 2002 (Pub L. 107-204) was passed in response to the ENRON and WorldCom frauds (See Figure 5.14 above). Section 906 of the law requires that a company's CEO and CFO both sign a written statement that accompanies the financial statements. The officers are required to certify that the financial statements fully comply with the requirements of the Securities Exchange Act of 1934 and that information contained in the periodic annual report fairly presents, in all material respects, the financial condition and results of operations of the issuer. The second part of this statement is the anti-fraud provision. If the officers willfully sign the certification knowing that it is false then they are subject to a file of not more than $5 million and/or imprisonment of not more than 20 years.

Conclusion

In this chapter we have looked at several different tools for financial statement analysis including ratio analysis, trend analysis and common-sized financial statements. These tools are useful to help us understand the stories told by financial statements, and if we use them carefully, to uncover fraud indicators or red flags if they exist. In the final chapter we are going to look at some of the accounting choices that companies make. These choices affect the amounts that are disclosed on financial statements. In addition, these choices make comparing the financial statements of different companies, even in the same industry, more difficult when the companies in question make different accounting choices.

Chapter 6

Accounting Choices and Financial Statements

Many people view accounting as an exact science. It's not. Accounting is a pragmatic art or a social science, and one where the artist, the accountant, is able to make many decisions that affect the results shown on the financial statements. As a social science accounting seeks to find ways to help decision makers make better decision by providing relevant and reliable information. This chapter discusses some of the more common areas where accountants are able to choose between alternative accounting treatments and thus influence the reported results of operations, financial position, and cash flow of the company.

In this chapter we will look at accounting decisions related to reporting short-term investments, the net realizable value of accounts receivable, inventory valuation, depreciation and leases. These are all areas where accountants are able to elect between different accounting treatments. As we look at these different areas pay particular attention to the effect of alternative accounting treatments on the financial statements.

Choices, in accounting?!?!?! I don't want to make choices!

Short-term Investments

You should recall that assets are usually valued at historical cost on a balance sheet. Accounting for short-term investments is one of the areas where GAAP departs from the historical cost principle. Short-term investments are investments in stock and bonds, for the most part, that a company expects to hold for less than a year. Cash in the bank in a checking account represents assets that are not being used; the cash is just sitting there and is not generating revenue. Consequently many companies purchase stock and bonds as a way to invest cash and earn revenue. They will hold on to those investments until the cash is needed, at which point the investments are sold (hopefully for a profit). The value of stocks and bonds in an investment portfolio can be determined at any time without selling the assets because of the existence of securities markets. Thus accounting principles allow (require) that short-term investments be accounted for differently (not through the use of the historical cost principle).

Short-term investments can be classified as (1) trading securities, (2) available-for-sale securities, and (3) held-to-maturity securities. Held-to-maturity securities are bonds because bonds have a maturity date, stock does not. Held-to-maturity securities are reported at amortized cost. This means that they are reported on the balance sheet at their face value plus any premium paid to purchase the bond, or less any discount realized on the purchase. The premium or discount is reduced, on a percentage basis, every year and the change is reported as a decrease or increase in revenue earned on the bond.

For example, assume that a company invests in a five-year, $100,000, 10% bond and pays a $2,000 premium to purchase the bond. At the date of purchase the bond would be valued on the balance sheet at $102,000. Every year the company will earn 10 percent interest, or $10,000, on the bond. In addition, let's assume that the company uses simple straight line amortization to account for the premium on the bond. That means that every year 20 percent (1/term of bond or 1/5) of the premium will be written off against revenue on the bond. The following table shows what happens to the bond over the five year period.

Table 6.1
Bond Amortization

Year	Beginning Value	Interest Received	Premium Amortization	Reported Revenue	End of Year Value
1	$102,000	$10,000	$ 400	$9,600	$101,600
2	$101,600	$10,000	$ 400	$9,600	$101,200
3	$101,200	$10,000	$ 400	$9,600	$100,800
4	$100,800	$10,000	$ 400	$9,600	$100,400
5	$100,400	$10,000	$ 400	$9,600	$100,000

Notice that the balance sheet value of the bond decreases from its purchase price, $102,000 to its face value of $100,000 at maturity. The reduction (amortization) of the bond premium reduced the amount or revenue reported on the income statement from the $10,000 cash received to $9,600. The amortization of a discount would have the opposite effect. This should make good economic sense. In the above case the company paid $102,000 for an investment that paid $10,000 interest per year. This means that the company was earning slightly less than 10 percent on its investment and this is reflected in the lower reported revenue. In fact, the company was actually earning 9.8 percent ($10,000 / $102,000) on their initial investment. A bond discount would have the opposite effect. Amortization of the discount would increase interest revenue.

Held-to-Maturity Securities

While held-to-maturity securities are interesting, they don't provide the same opportunity to affect the income statement as do trading securities and available-for-sale securities. Assume that a company invested $1,000,000 of excess cash in GM stock. Should that investment be reported as a trading security or an available for sale security, and does it make a difference? The answer to the first question is "It depends." and the answer to the second question is "Yes!".

Available for Sale and Trading Securities

The classification of the investment of GM stock is *totally* dependent on management's intent. If they are going to flip the investment quickly because they think that the price of GM stock is going to increase then the investment is an investment in a trading security. On the other hand, if they are going to hold onto the investment until the time is right to sell it then it is an available-for-sale security. Management's intent is the key.

In both cases the investment will be reported on the balance sheet at market value at year end. Assume that the value of the $1,000,000 investment in GM stock had increased to $1,200,000 at year end. The investment would be reported at $1,200,000 on the balance sheet. That means that there is a $200,000 increase in value (a holding gain) that needs to be reported. If management's intent is to hold the stock as a trading security then that gain will be reported on the income statement, increasing net income. On the other hand if, again based on management's intent, the investment is classified as an available-for-sale security then the gain would bypass the income statement and be reported in other comprehensive income in the equity section of the balance sheet. Net income would be unaffected by the holding gain. Holding losses would be reported the same way.

> Unrealized Holding Gains and Losses: Increases or decreases in value resulting from holding an asset in a period of changing prices. Holding gains and losses are unrealized because the asset has not been sold but may be reported on financial statements at current market value.

Assume that you are corporate VP of Finance and your company invested $2,000,000 in the stock market and prices have declined, resulting in a $500,000 holding loss. Where would you like that loss to appear, on the income statement, or hidden in other comprehensive income on the balance sheet? If you can classify the stock as an available-for-sale investment you can move the loss directly to the equity section of the balance sheet and the income statement will be unaffected by the loss. This simple choice can have, in this case, a $500,000 effect on the income statement.

Accounts Receivable

A reporting objective for accounts receivable is to show the net realizable value of accounts receivable on the balance sheet. This means that a company should disclose not how much customers owe the company but rather how much the company reasonably expects to collect from the customers. A contra-asset account, Allowance for Uncollectible Accounts, is used to adjust accounts receivable from book value to net realizable value.

> Contra-account: An account that is used to adjust the balance of a related account. The contra account has the opposite sign of the account that it is adjusting. Thus, because assets have normal debit balances, a contra-asset account would have a normal credit balance.

The balance sheet disclosure of accounts receivable is (with assumed numbers):

Accounts Receivable	$200,000
Less Allowance for Uncollectible Accounts	(15,000)
Accounts Receivable, Net	$185,000

In this example customers owe the company $200,000 but the company only expects to be able to collect $185,000 of the total amount owed. Often times you will only see the net accounts receivable amount disclosed on the balance sheet. The allowance account amount will then be found in one of the footnotes to the financial statements.

The opportunity to manipulate the financial statements occurs in the way that the allowance account balance is computed. The two approaches to estimating bad debts and the allowance account balance are (1) the income statement approach, and (2) the balance sheet approach. In the income statement approach bad debt expense is estimated as a percentage of sales, and the estimated expense amount is added to the balance in the allowance account.

In the balance sheet approach the ending balance in the allowance account is estimated as a percentage of accounts receivable. The bad debt expense and the adjustment to the allowance account are computed as the difference between the current balance in the allowance account and the computed desired ending balance.

Let's assume the following set of facts:

- Sales — $1,000,000
- Accounts Receivable balance — $ 200,000
- Allowance for Uncollectible Accounts balance — $ 2,000
- Bad Debt Expense — 3% of sales,
  or
- Allowance for Uncollectible Accounts accounts receivable — 15% of

If the company uses the income statement approach then bad debt expense would be computed as 3 percent of sales, or $30,000. Bad debt expense of $30,000 would be reported on the income statement and $30,000 would be added to the balance in the allowance for uncollectible accounts account giving it an ending balance of $32,000.

Had the company used the balance sheet approach (percentage of accounts receivable) it would first have computed the desired ending balance in the allowance account as 15 percent of accounts receivable, or $30,000. The current balance in the allowance account is $2,000 so to adjust from $2,000 to $30,000 the company needs to add $28,000 to the allowance account. This would also result in $28,000 being reported as bad debt expense on the income statement.

Company management has to make two decisions. The first decision is to decide which method to use and second decision is to select the percentages to use in the calculations. The income statement approach is theoretically superior because it is motived by the principle of matching revenues and expenses in the same accounting period (the matching principle) by basing the calculation of the bad debt expense on revenue generated. The balance sheet approach may be pragmatically superior because management can analyze the individual accounts that make up accounts receivable to better estimate the uncollectible accounts.

Top management and auditors often have lengthy discussion about the appropriate percentages. Management has an incentive to minimize the expense and the allowance account balance by using low percentages. Auditors, have an incentive, because of conservatism, to estimate the percentages on the high end of the range of reasonable estimations. An opportunity to negotiate is also an opportunity to manipulate the financial statements.

Inventory Valuation

Assume that a company made the following purchases of product AB1950:

Purchase Date	Quantity Purchased	Unit Cost Cost
Jan 15	100	$1.00
March 12	100	$1.10
June 29	100	$1.15
Oct. 1	100	$1.20

The company had 400 units available to sell and those units cost a total of $445. Further assume that over the course of the year the company sold 250 units for $10.00 each, ending the year with 150 units on hand. Revenue from the sale of AB1950 is easy to compute, its $2,500 (250 units x $10.00 per unit). But what was cost of goods sold?

The answer is, once again, it depends. It depends on the cost-flow assumption that the company makes. The four common cost-flow assumptions are:

- Specific identification,
- First In, First Out (FIFO),
- Last In, Last Out (LIFO), and
- Weighted Average

Specific Identification

Specific identification is used when individual items can be directly associated with their respective costs, making it possible to match the item sold with its cost. This means that technically the specific identification method is not a cost-flow assumption. Probably the best example of this is an auto dealership. The dealership knows the cost of every vehicle on its lot and when a car is sold can identify the unique cost of that car. Specific identification doesn't work well when products are homogeneous and may have been purchased at different times with different costs.

Use Specific Identification with Heterogeneous Products

FIFO

First In First Out (FIFO) describes the cost flow assumption in which the first items placed in inventory are assumed to be the first item sold. Let's take a look at the purchase information presented above. Recall that 250 units were sold. We can identify the *inventory layers* from which those items were sold, starting with the oldest layer (because we are doing FIFO) as follows in Table 6.2.

Table 6.2
FIFO Cost Flow Calculations

Purchase Date	Quantity Purchased	Unit Cost Cost	Units Sold	Units in Ending Inventory
Jan 15	100	$1.00	100	
March 12	100	$1.10	100	
June 29	100	$1.15	50	50
Oct. 1	100	$1.20	0	100
Totals	400 units		250 units	150 units

The costs associated with the first 100 units sold come from the January 15 purchase, the costs for the next 100 units sold come from the March 12 purchase and half (50 units) of the June 29 purchase were sold. This means that the other 50 units purchase on June 29 are still in inventory at the end of the period along will all of the units from the October 1 purchase.

Cost of goods sold is computed as 100($1.00) + 100($1.10) + 50($1.15) or $267.50. We can compute ending inventory the same way: 50($1.15) + 100($1.20) or $177.50.

LIFO

Last In First Out (LIFO) makes the opposite assumption. That is, that the last units purchased are assumed to be the first units sold. Let's analyze the purchase layers again, this time with a LIFO cost-flow assumption.

This time the costs associated with the first 100 units sold come from the October 1 purchase, the costs for the next 100 units sold come from the June 29 purchase and half (50 units) of the March 12 purchase are assumed to have been sold. This means that the other 50 units purchased on March 12 are still in inventory at the end of the period along will all of the units from the January 15 purchase.

Table 6.3
LIFO Cost Flow Calculations

Purchase Date	Quantity Purchased	Unit Cost Cost	Units Sold	Units in Ending Inventory
Jan 15	100	$1.00	0	100
March 12	100	$1.10	50	50
June 29	100	$1.15	100	0
Oct. 1	100	$1.20	100	0
Totals	400 units		250 units	150 units

Cost of goods sold is computed as 100($1.20) + 100($1.15) + 50($1.10) or $290.00. We can compute ending inventory the same way: 50($1.10) + 100($1.00) or $155.00.

Weighted Average

As you will see below, the weighted average cost-flow assumption is a compromise between FIFO and LIFO. To compute cost of goods sold and ending inventory using the weighted average method we first need to compute a weighted average cost per unit. We do this by dividing the cost of goods available for sale by the number of units available for sale:

$$Weighted\ Average\ Cost\ per\ Unit = \frac{Goods\ Available\ for\ Sale\ \$}{Units\ Available\ for\ Sale}$$

Goods available for sale and units available for sale are computed below in Table 6.4.

Table 6.4
Weighted Average Cost Flow Calculations

Purchase Date	Quantity Purchased	x	Unit Cost Cost	=	Total Cost
Jan 15	100		$1.00		$100.00
March 12	100		$1.10		$110.00
June 29	100		$1.15		$115.00
Oct. 1	<u>100</u>		$1.20		<u>$120.00</u>
Units Available for Sale 400					
Goods Available for Sale $					$445.00

So the weighted average cost per unit is:

$$Weighted\ Average\ Cost\ per\ Unit = \frac{Goods\ Available\ for\ Sale\ \$}{Units\ Available\ for\ Sale}$$

$$= \frac{\$445.00}{400} = \$1.1125$$

Ending inventory and cost of goods sold are the product of the number of units in ending inventory (or the number of units sold) times the weighted average cost per unit.

For our example they are computed as:

Ending Inventory   = 150 units ($1.1125) = $166.88

Cost of Goods Sold = 250 units ($1.1125) = $278.12 (rounded down)

Comparison

Now we can compare what happens with FIFO, LIFO and weighted average and start to discuss the advantages of each method. The comparative cost of goods sold section below summarizes our calculations.

Table 6.5
Comparative Cost of Goods Sold Calculations
FIFO, Weighted Average, and FIFO

	FIFO	Weighted Average	LIFO
Beginning Inventory	$ 0.00	$ 0.00	$ 0.00
Purchases	445.00	445.00	445.00
Goods Available for Sale	445.00	445.00	445.00
Less Ending Inventory	(177.50)	(166.88)	(155.00)
Cost of Goods Sold	$ 267.50	$278.12	$290.00

First, notice that both the value of ending inventory and cost of goods sold, when computed using the weighted average method, fall between the FIFO and LIFO value. The weight average method is a compromise. And like may compromises, it doesn't do anything really well.

FIFO, in a period of rising prices, results in a higher ending inventory value than does LIFO. That is because under the FIFO method the most recent inventory purchases are in ending inventory and the items acquired at earlier dates and which have lower unit costs are allocated to cost of goods sold. You might want to remember that FIFO = LIST or First-In, First-Out also means Last-In, Still-There. As a result FIFO presents the "best" financial picture of ending inventory on the balance sheet. The balance sheet is a picture of a company's financial position at a point in time. FIFO, in periods of rising prices, gives the most realistic picture of the financial position or the best estimate of the replacement cost value of the company's inventory.

LIFO on the other hand, again in a period of rising prices, results in higher cost of goods sold than does FIFO. This is because the most recent inventory costs appear on the income statement as cost of goods sold when LIFO is used. You might want to remember that LIFO = FIST or Last-In, First-Out also means First-In, Still-There. This has two important effects. First, because cost of goods sold is higher under LIFO than it would have been under FIFO, LIFO gross profit and consequently net income are lower than they would have been had FIFO been used.

You might logically ask yourself why would a company want to minimize its net income? The answer is *taxes*. By minimizing net income through the adoption of the LIFO method a company minimizes the cash outflow for taxes. To see how that works, let's take a look at a simple example. We will assume the following:

- Sales (all cash) $1,000,000
- Cash payment for inventory $ 700,000
- FIFO Cost of goods sold $ 500,000
- LIFO Cost of goods sold $ 600,000
- Other expenses (all cash) $ 100,000
- Tax rate   35%

Now we can prepare comparative income statements using FIFO and LIFO in Table 6.6.

Table 6.6
Sample Company
FIFO and LIFO Comparative Income Statements
For the Year Ended December 31, 2013

	FIFO	LIFO
Revenue	$1,000,000	$1,000,000
Cost of goods sold	(500,000)	(600,000)
Gross profit	$ 500,000	$ 400,000
Operating expenses	(100,000)	(100,000)
Income before taxes	$ 400,000	300,000
Income tax expense	(140,000)	(105,000)
Net income	$ 260,000	$ 195,000

Obviously FIFO is better, right? After all FIFO net income is $65,000 higher than LIFO net income. As the info commercials say, "But wait!" What about cash flow. The following shows an analysis of cash flow from operations under both FIFO and LIFO.

Table 6.7
Sample Company
FIFO and LIFO Comparative Cash Flow from Operations
For the Year Ended December 31, 2013

	FIFO	LIFO
Cash collected from customers	$1,000,000	$1,000,000
Cash paid for inventory	(700,000)	(700,000)
Cash paid for operating expenses	(100,000)	(100,000)
Cash paid for taxes	(140,000)	(105,000)
Cash provided by operations	$ 60,000	$ 95,000

It's true that net income, again in periods of rising prices, is higher under FIFO than it would be under LIFO, it's also true that a company that uses LIFO will pay less in taxes and have higher cash flow. Notice in Table 6.7 that the only difference in cash flow from operations was cash paid for taxes. While net income is nice, you can't pay the bills with net income, you pay the bills with cash and LIFO minimizes cash outflow, the second effect of using LIFO.

Note that the Internal Revenue Code requires that if a company uses LIFO for financial reporting that it must also use LIFO for computing its tax liability.

Once again, the choice of an accounting practice can have a significant effect on the financial statements. Most of the significant accounting choices that a company makes are disclosed in the first footnote to the financial statements.

Depreciation

Income determination, as discussed in Chapter 1, has two components, revenue recognition and expense matching. Matching is the process of assigning business expenses to specific accounting periods. The general concept is that revenues and expenses should be matched together and recognized in the same accounting period. In theory there are three ways to match expenses to revenues:

- Cause and effect matching,
- Systematic and rational allocation, and
- Immediate recognition.

Cause and effect matching is used when specific activities[5] and the costs that they incur can be traced to unique revenue-generating transactions. For example, the activities of salespeople have a cost (sales commissions) and their activities lead to sales (revenue) so we can match sales commission with the revenue generated in cause and effect manner in the same accounting period.

Sometimes the expenditure of resources (cash) or the incurrence of a debt (liability) leads to the acquisition of an asset that will provide economic benefits over more than one accounting period. When that happens the cost of the asset is systematically and rationally allocated to the accounting periods that benefit from the use of the asset. For example, let's assume the following facts for a small pizzeria:

- Annual revenue: $100,000
- Annual operating expenses $ 55,000

The owner of the pizzeria decides to start offering delivery services and purchases a used delivery truck for $32,000. The truck is expected to have a four-year useful life and no residual value.

---

[5] All activities have associates costs, however not all activities add value. A good manager identifies and eliminates non-value-adding activities (and their associated costs).

> Residual Value: The expected value of an
> asset at the end of its useful life.

If annual revenue and operating expenses don't change, and the purchase of the truck is recorded as expense in year 1, the year when the truck was purchased, then comparative income statements for the first five years will show the following:

Table 6.8
Pizzeria
Comparative Income Statements
For the Years Ended December 31, Years 1 through 5

	Year 1	Year 2	Year 3	Year 4	Total
Revenue	$100,000	$100,000	$100,000	$100,000	$400,000
Operating Expense	(55,000)	(55,000)	(55,000)	(55,000)	(20,000)
Truck Expense	(32,000)	0	0	0	(32,000)
Pre-tax Net Income	$ 13,000	$ 45,000	$ 45,000	$ 45,000	$148,000

Notice how year 1 was penalized by the purchase of the truck? It bore the entire cost of the truck, even though years 2, 3 and 4 benefited from the use of the truck. By depreciating the truck, by systematically and rationally allocating the cost of the truck over the years the benefit from its use, we can spread the cost of the truck out, and more accurately measure net income each year.

Straight-line Deprecation

The easiest way to depreciate the truck is to divide the cost of the truck, less any residual value, by the life of the truck. We subtract the residual value because that is a recoverable cost and so it should not be treated as an expense. This method of computing depreciation is called *straight-line depreciation*. The formula for computing the annual straight-line depreciation expense is:

$$Annual\ Straight - Line\ Depreciation\ Expense =$$
$$= \frac{Asset\ Cost - Residual\ Value}{Estimated\ Useful\ Life}$$

For the delivery tuck purchased by the pizzeria we would compute straight-line depreciation as:

$$Annual\ Straight - Line\ Depreciation\ Expense =$$

$$= \frac{Asset\ Cost - Residual\ Value}{Estimated\ Useful\ Life}$$

$$= \frac{\$32,000 - 0}{4} = \$8,000$$

Table 6.9 below repeats the income statement for the pizzeria using straight line depreciation.

Table 6.9
Pizzeria
Comparative Income Statements
For the Years Ended December 31, Years 1 through 5

	Year 1	Year 2	Year 3	Year 4	Total
Revenue	$100,000	$100,000	$100,000	$100,000	$400,000
Operating Expense	(55,000)	(55,000)	(55,000)	(55,000)	(20,000)
Depreciation Expense	(8,000)	(8,000)	(8,000)	(8,000)	(32,000)
Pre-tax Net Income	$ 37,000	$ 37,000	$ 37,000	$ 37,000	$148,000

Notice, by comparing tables 6.8 and 6.9, that cumulative, four-year net income in both cases is $148,000. That is because the expenses were the same in both case, they were just recognized in different periods.

Straight-line deprecation is called "straight line" because the depreciation expense is constant over time. In Table 6.9 it was $8,000 per year, year after year.

Depreciation is recorded by increasing the expense account, depreciation expense (with a debit) and by increasing the contra-asset account accumulated depreciation (with a credit). Accumulated depreciation, like other contra-asset accounts, reduces the balance of an associated asset account from historical cost to net book value. In the case of the pizza delivery truck that cost $32,000 the balance sheet disclosure at the end of year one would be:

Delivery Truck $32,000 ◄━━━ Historical cost
Less Accumulated Depreciation (8,000)
Delivery Truck, net $24,000 ◄━━━ Book value

At the end of the second year the balance sheet would show the following:

Delivery Truck $32,000
Less Accumulated Depreciation (16,000)
Delivery Truck, net $16,000

You should be able to see that at the end of the assets useful life the book value on the balance sheet would be equal to the asset's residual value.

Units of Production Depreciation

A depreciation method that is similar to the straight-line method, and which does a better job of cause-and-effect matching is units-of-production deprecation. In units-of-production (UP) depreciation the useful life of the asset is measured by expected life-time productive capacity rather than time. Units-of-production depreciation is a two-step process. In the first step a depreciation rate per unit produced is computed. In the second step, that rate is used to compute annual depreciation expense based on actual production. The UP rate is computed as:

$$UP\ Rate = \frac{Cost - Residual\ Value}{Estimated\ Lifetime\ Production}$$

and annual deprecation is computed as:

$$Annual\ UP\ Depreciation\ Expense = (Actual\ Production)\ (UP\ Rate)$$

Let's assume that the Pizzeria's delivery truck is expected to provide 100,000 miles of useful service over its four year life and that the truck was driven 20,000 miles in the first year and 30,000 miles the second year. The UP Rate is:

$$UP\ Rate = \frac{Cost - Residual\ Value}{Estimated\ Lifetime\ Production}$$

$$UP\ Rate = \frac{(\$32,000 - 0)}{100,000\ miles} = \$0.32/mile$$

Depreciation expense for years 1 and 2 would be computed as:

$$Annual\ UP\ Depreciation\ Expense = (Actual\ Production)\ (UP\ Rate)$$

$$Year\ 1\ UP\ Depreciation\ Expense = (20,000)(\$0.32) = \$6,400$$

$$Year\ 2\ UP\ Depreciation\ Expense = (30,000)(\$0.32) = \$9,600$$

In straight-line depreciation the annual depreciation expense was constant over time. When UP deprecation is used the UP Rate is constant over time.

Accelerated Deprecation

For reasons that will be discussed below, many companies use accelerated deprecation methods. These methods do not result in constant depreciation expenses over time but rather higher depreciation in the early years of an asset's life. In other words, depreciation expense is accelerated to the early years of the asset's life.

One of the most common forms of accelerated depreciation is *double-declining balance* depreciation. Recall that the straight-line deprecation rate can be expressed as:

$$Straight - Line\ Depreciation\ Rate = \frac{1}{Estimated\ Useful\ Life}$$

Thus an asset with a 4 year life is depreciated at 25 percent (1/4 = 0.25 = 25 percent) per year. Double-declining balance depreciation uses a depreciation rate that is twice the straight line rate. Thus:

$$Double - declining\ Balance\ Depreciation\ Rate =$$
$$= 2\ x\ \frac{1}{Estimated\ Useful\ Life}$$
$$= \frac{2}{Estimated\ Useful\ Life}$$

This means that an asset with a four year estimated useful life would be depreciated at 50 percent per year (2 x ¼ = 0.50 = 50 percent). Obviously if we depreciate an asset at the rate of 50 percent per year it will be fully depreciated at the end of two, not four, years. That's where the declining balance comes in. Double declining balance depreciation is not computed as a percentage of historical cost, like we did with straight-line depreciation. Rather, it is computed on the basis of the asset's book value at the beginning of the year.

$$Book\ Value = Historical\ Cost - Accumulated\ Depreciation$$

It should be obvious that historical cost is equal to book value at the beginning of the first year of an asset's life because accumulated depreciation would be zero.

The following table shows the computation of depreciation expense and accumulated depreciation for the pizza delivery truck.

Table 6.12
Double-declining Balance Deprecation

Year	Historical Cost	BOY Acum. Depr.	BOY Book Value	Depr. Rate	Dep Expense	EOY Acum. Depr.
1	$32,000	$0	$32,000	0.50	$16,000	$16,000
2	$32,000	$16,000	$16,000	0.50	$ 8,000	$24,000
3	$32,000	$24,000	$ 8,000	0.50	$ 4,000	$28,000
4	$32,000	$28,000	$ 4,000		$ 1,000	$29,000

Note:

Acum. Depr. = Accumulated Depreciation
BOY = Beginning of Year
Depr. = Depreciation
EOY = End of Year

First, a couple of observations about Table 6.10 and then we will discover a problem with our calculations. Note that historical cost never changes. Beginning-of-year (BOY) accumulated depreciation for year one is zero; the asset has not been depreciated so there is no accumulated depreciation. After year one, beginning-of-year accumulated depreciation is equal to the end-of-year (EOY) accumulated depreciation from the prior year. That is to say, accumulated depreciation at the end of year 1 becomes beginning-of-year accumulated depreciation for year 2.

Every year BOY book value is equal to historical cost less the beginning of year accumulated depreciation. Depreciation expense is computed by multiplying BOY book value by the depreciation rate. EOY accumulated depreciation is equal to BOY accumulated depreciation plus current year depreciation expense.

Now for the problem. Our asset had a residual value of zero yet at the end of year 4 the book value, in Table 6.10, is $2,000 (historical cost of $32,000 less EOY accumulated depreciation of $30,000). This often happens with double-declining balance depreciation. The solution is to ignore the depreciation formula in the last year of the assets life (or sometimes a year or two earlier) and plug in a number for depreciation expense that will result in an EOY book value that is equal to the asset's residual value. That has been done in Table 6.11 below.

Table 6.11

Double-declining Balance Deprecation

Year	Historical Cost	BOY Acum. Depr.	BOY Book Value	Depr. Rate	Dep Expense	EOY Acum. Depr.
1	$32,000	$0	$32,000	0.50	$16,000	$16,000
2	$32,000	$16,000	$16,000	0.50	$ 8,000	$24,000
3	$32,000	$24,000	$ 8,000	0.50	$ 4,000	$28,000
4	$32,000	$28,000	$ 4,000		$ 4,000	$32,000

Now that we have ignored the deprecation rate in year 4 and plugged in $4,000 for depreciation expense in year 4 the ending accumulated depreciation is equal to $32,000, the same as the value of the historical cost, so the asset is fully depreciated with no residual value. This shown in the following calculation:

Delivery Truck	$ 32,000
Less Accumulated Depreciation	($ 32,000)
Delivery Truck, net	$ -0-

What would you do if the asset had an estimated residual value of $3,000 instead of zero? Give it a little thought and then take a look at Table 6.12.

Table 6.12

Double-declining Balance Deprecation

Year	Historical Cost	BOY Acum. Depr.	BOY Book Value	Depr. Rate	Dep Expense	EOY Acum. Depr.
1	$32,000	$0	$32,000	0.50	$16,000	$16,000
2	$32,000	$16,000	$16,000	0.50	$ 8,000	$24,000
3	$32,000	$24,000	$ 8,000	0.50	$ 4,000	$28,000
4	$32,000	$28,000	$ 4,000		$ 1,000	$29,000

Now at the end of year 4 the balance sheet would show:

Delivery Truck	$32,000
Less Accumulated Depreciation	(29,000)
Delivery Truck, net	$ 3,000

and the net book value of the delivery truck is equal to the estimated residual value.

The Internal Revenue Code uses as deprecation method called MACRS (Modified Accelerated Cost Recovery System). This system is similar to double-declining balance depreciation, but with a depreciation rate computed at 1.5 or 2 times the straight-line rate, depending on the asset class. MACRS depreciation also makes some assumptions about when an asset is placed in service. The most common assumption is that all assets were placed in service at mid-year so MACRS allows one-half year's depreciation expense in the first year of an asset's life and an additional one-half year in the year following the last year of an asset's life. That means that an asset with a five year life is depreciated over six years, with one-half year's depreciation taken the first year and one-half year's depreciation taken the sixth year. Many companies use MACRS for both financial reporting and tax purposes.

There are two important reasons why companies elect to use an accelerate depreciation method. First is the time-value of money. Depreciation expense is a non-cash, tax-deductible expense. No one writes a check to "pay" for depreciation, but the expense reduces tax obligations. One dollar today is worth more than one dollar a year, or five years, from now (the time value of money). Consequently a tax deduction in the current year is also worth more than a tax deduction in the future. Accelerated depreciation moves the tax deductions for depreciation expense into the early years of an asset's life when the purchasing power of the dollar is expected to be greater.

The second reason is to smooth out the cost of ownership. As an asset ages, its associated repair and maintenance costs increase. If you have ever driven a ten-year-old car you know that repair costs increase with age. The two components of the total cost of ownership of an asset are depreciation expense and repair and maintenance expenses. Figure 6.1 below depicts these costs when straight-line depreciation is used.

Figure 6.1
Total Cost of Ownership Assuming Straight-line Depreciation

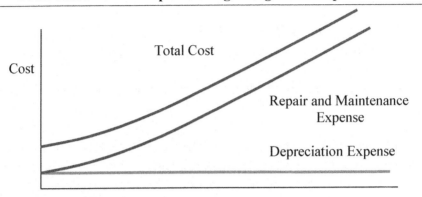

Notice in Figure 6.1 that the total cost of ownership increases with time. Figure 6.2 shows what happens to the total cost of ownership when accelerated deprecation is used.

Figure 6.2
Total Cost of Ownership Assuming Accelerate Depreciation

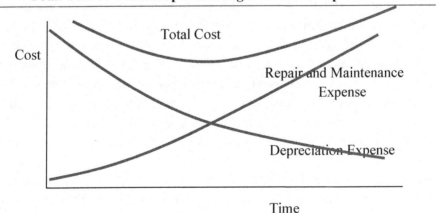

While the total cost of ownership may not be constant over time when accelerated depreciation is used, it is much flatter (smoother) than with straight-line deprecation.

Financial Statement Implications

The choice of a deprecation method affects all of the financial statements. Depreciation expense affects the income statement, and consequently the statement of changes in stockholder equity or statement of retained earnings. The balance sheet is affected by accumulated depreciation in the asset section and depreciation expense in the stockholders' equity section. Finally the statement of cash flows includes the cash outflow for the payment of taxes, which can be affected by the deprecation method choice, depreciation expenses is excluded from the computation of cash provided by operations. These differences are all timing differences because total depreciation expense and consequently total accumulated depreciation will be the same over time, regardless of the depreciation method chosen.

Amortization and Depletion

Fixed assets (property, plant and equipment) are depreciated. Intangible assets like patents, copyrights and trademarks are amortized over their expected economic lives using a method that is identical to straight-line depreciation. The only difference is that the value of the asset is reduced directly when amortization expense is recorded; no accumulated amortization account is used.

Natural resources are depleted. The depletion calculation is essentially the same as that used for units-of-production depreciation. The cost of the natural resource is divided by expected production (barrels of oil for example in an oil well) to compute a depletion cost per unit. This is then multiplied by the number of units produced in a period to compute depletion expense. Like the amortization of intangible assets, the value of the natural resource is reduced directly when depletion is recorded.

Leases

A lease is a contractual arrangement calling for the lessee (user) to pay the lessor (owner) for use of an asset, usually for a specific period of time. Surprisingly this is an area where by carefully structuring the lease contract a company have been able to affect financial statement presentation of leased assets and lease obligations. We are going to restrict our attention to the accounting treatment of leases by the lessee.

On February 25, 2016, the Financial Accounting Standards Board (FASB) issued an Accounting Standards Update (ASU). This updated was designed to improve financial reporting about leasing transactions. Before the issuance of the ASU some leases were classified as capital leases (for example, a lease of equipment for nearly all of its useful life).

When a lease was classified as a capital lease companies were required to recognize the leased assets and corresponding liabilities on the balance sheet. Other leases were classified as operating leases. Expenses for operating leases, essentially rent expense, appear on the income statement. A company could carefully structure a lease agreement so that he requirements for the lease to be treated as a capital lease were not triggered, and this provided an opportunity for off-balance-sheet financing.

Financial Accounting Standard 13 required that a lease be accounted for as a capital lease if *any one* of the following criteria is met:

1. Ownership of the asset transfers from the lessor to the lessee at the end of the lease term, or
2. The lease agreement includes a bargain purchase option giving the lessee the right to purchase the asset (usually at the end of the lease term) for less than fair market value, or
3. The lease term is equal to or greater than 75 percent of the expected useful life of the asset, or
4. The present value of the lease payments is equal to or greater than 90 percent of the cost of the asset.

These rules give company management the ability to structure a lease transaction so that the asset and corresponding obligation either do or do not appear on the financial statements of the lessee. This is one way to accomplish off-balance-sheet financing.

The treatment of some leases as operating leases was criticized because it resulted in financial statements that failed to meet the needs of users of financial statements. Essentially it did not always provide a faithful representation of leasing transactions and lead to form-over-substance issues.

The new standard requires that organizations that lease assets, the "lessees", recognize leased assets and the corresponding liabilities on the balance sheet for all leases with a term of more than 12 months. This means that both capital and operating leases will be presented on the balance sheet.

The new ASU also requires disclosures to help investors and other financial statement users better understand the amount, timing, and uncertainty of cash flows arising from leases. These disclosures include qualitative and quantitative requirements, providing additional information about the amounts recorded in the financial statements.

The new ASU is effective for public companies for fiscal years, and interim periods within those fiscal years, beginning after December 15, 2018. Thus, for a calendar year public company, it would be effective January 1, 2019. The ASU will take effect for all other organizations for fiscal years beginning after December 15, 2019 and for interim periods within fiscal years beginning after December 15, 2020.

The change in GAAP to better present the economic substance of lease transactions is an example of the way that GAAP evolves over time. It also highlights the need for accountants and users of financial statements to stay current with changes in promulgated GAAP.

Conclusion

In this chapter we have reviewed some of the more obvious and important decisions which accountants and auditors make about the numbers that appear on financial statements. While the choices are often pragmatic they really should be theory driven. The accounting methods used should provide users of financial statements with information that is relevant and reliable, and which promotes within-firm consistency and between-firm comparability.

It seems appropriate to end this little book at this point. You will recall that accounting standards and the standards setting process was discussed in chapter one. You have now seen an example of that process in action.

Accounting will continue to evolve as the needs of financial statement users change, and as business transactions become more complex and more global. Stick around, the ride will be fun.

INDEX

Accelerated deprecation 158, 166

Accounting 6

Accounting equation 20, 21, 22, 23, 25, 40, 41, 42, 43, 44, 47, 48, 49, 50, 71, 75, 116

Accounts receivable management 112

Accounts Receivable Turnover 108, 110

Accrual accounting 60, 61, 67, 91

Accumulated depreciation 54, 157, 159, 161, 163, 167

Acid-test ratio 28, 29

Allowance for Uncollectible Accounts 143

Amortization 167

Asset utilization ratios 108

Assets ..20, 24, 25, 39, 41, 42, 43, 44, 45, 46, 50, 68, 70, 72, 74, 75, 88, 97, 105, 106, 107, 109, 111, 118, 120, 121

Available-for-sale securities 140, 141

Average Collection Period 108, 109, 110, 111

Average Days in Inventory 109, 111

Balance sheet9, 19, 20, 21, 22, 23, 24, 25, 26, 27, 28, 32, 33, 34, 37, 38, 40, 41, 45, 54, 64, 68, 75, 76, 82, 88, 91, 92, 100, 127, 140, 141, 142, 143, 144, 145, 150, 157, 165, 167, 169

Balance sheet approach 144

Book value 54

Cash Flow Statement 86

Classified Balance Sheet 39

Closing 80

Common sized 59

Common sized financial statements 127

Common stock 33

Comparability 14

Comparative data 102

Conservatism 12

Consistency 14

Constraints 11

Contra-account 143

Credit 48

Current assets 20

Current Liabilities to Inventory 106, 107

Current Liabilities to Owners' Equity 106, 107

Current ratio 28, 29, 107

Current Ratio 30, 105, 107

Days to Make Payables 110, 112

Debit 48

Debt to Equity Ratio 117, 118

Debt to Total Assets 117

Depletion 167

Depreciation 59

Direct method 91

Double entry accounting 50

Double-declining balance depreciation 159, 161, 165

Dupont Analysis 121

Earnings per share 65

Earnings per Share (Basic) 119, 120

Entity concept 14

Estimated Operating Cycle 109, 111

Expense 54

Extraordinary items 63

FASB 4, 5, 7, 8, 10, 15

FIFO.. 146, See First In, First Out

Financial Accounting Standards Board 5, 7

Financial position 24

Financing activities 87

First In, First Out... 146

Fraud 131, 132, 134, 136, 137, 138

Fraudulent financial reporting 132, 134, 137

Full-disclosure.. 16

GAAP....4, 5, 7, 8, 14, 27, 64, See Generally Accepted Accounting Principles

Generally Accepted Accounting Principles 4, 5

Going concern principle 14

Gross margin percentage 65

Gross profit 56

Gross profit percentage 57

Held-to-maturity securities.. 140, 141

Historical cost principle... 14, 16, 27, 140

Horizontal analysis...123

IASB ....See International Accounting Standards Board

IFRS.........................8, See International Financial Reporting Standards

Immediate recognition... 153

Income statement approach 144

Income taxes 63

Indirect method 91

Intangible assets 167

International Accounting Standards Board................................5, 8

International Financial Reporting Standards 8

Inventory Turnover 109, 110, 111

Investing activities 86

176

Journal entry 47, 50, 52, 77, 79

Last In, Last Out 146

Lease 27, 168

Leverage 30

Leverage Ratios 114

Liabilities 21

LIFO .... See Last In, First Out

MACRS .... See Modified Accelerated Cost Recovery System

Market capitalization 26

Matching 14, 16, 61, 94, 153, 157

Materiality 11

Modified Accelerated Cost Recovery System 165

Net asset 25

Net income 54

Net realizable value 143

Net worth 25

Neutral 13, 16

Operating activities 86

Operating cycle 113

Other income and expense 61

Owners' equity 21

Paid-in capital in excess of par 33

Par value 33

Periodicity 14, 15

Preferred stock 35

Price/earnings (P/E) ratio 66

Profit margin 65

Profit Margin 119, 120

Profitability ratios 118

Qualitative Characteristics 11

Quick Ratio 106, 107

Ratio analysis 105

Ratio of Accounts Payable to Sales 109, 110, 111, 112

Red flags 134

Relevance 13

Reliability 13

Representational faithfulness 13

Representationally faithful 13

Results of operations 54

Retained earnings 21, 33, 38, 71, 73, 75, 76, 79, 80, 82, 83, 119, 167

Return on Assets 119

Return on equity 116

Return on Equity 119, 120

Revenue principle 16

Revenue recognition 14, 17, 153

ROE .... See Return on Equity

Sale or disposal of a segment 62

Sarbanes-Oxley Act 137

SEC 4, 5, 7, 8

Securities and Exchange Commission 5, 7

Short-term investments 140

Short-term solvency ratios 105

Specific identification 146

Stable monetary unit assumption 14, 16

Stable-Monetary-Unit Assumption 15

Statement of Cash Flows 86

Statement of Retained Earnings 82

Statements of Financial Accounting Concepts 8

178

Straight-line depreciation 155, 158, 159, 165

Systematic and rational allocation 153

Times Interest Earned 117, 118

Total Asset Efficiency 109, 111

Trading securities 140, 141

Treasury stock 34, 35, 37

Unbiased 13

Understandability 11

Units-of-production 157

Verifiable 13, 16

Vertical analysis 127

Weighted Average 119, 146, 148, 149, 150

Working capital 28, 107

Working Capital 30, 105, 107, 109, 111

About the Author

 After graduating from Central Washington University in 1975 with a degree in accounting and a minor in computer science Dr. Murphy worked as a systems analyst, systems manager, and corporate controller. Some years later he graduated from Washington State University with an M.B.A and went to work for an international CPA firm as a senior IT consultant. That led to him starting his own CPA practice in Seattle, Washington.

Dr. Murphy was first licensed as a CPA in the State of Washington in 1981. Upon moving to Virginia he transferred his license to the Commonwealth of Virginia. In addition he was one of the first professional accountants certified in Kyrgyzstan. He is also a Certified Fraud Specialist and a member of the Board of Trustees of the Association of Certified Fraud Specialists. He has published over thirty articles in professional and academic journals in the United States and foreign countries and is a frequent speaker at conferences at workshops.

He eventually left his professional career and returned to Washington State University where he earned the first Ph. D. in accounting granted by WSU. After graduation he spent ten years on the faculty of a major state university, including a term as a Fulbright Fellow in Lima, Peru. That was followed by a number of years as an international development and anti-corruption consultant.

He spent over four years working in Bolivia, most of the time on an anti-corruption/graduate education project. He also served as chief-of-party on an accounting reform project in Central Asia, a year as the senior anti-corruption advisor to the Controller General of Peru, and as an anti-corruption advisor to the government of Bulgaria. He has also consulted on short-term anti-corruption engagements to other foreign governments.

He has worked as a higher education consultant in Mexico and Oman and more recently, to the State of Alabama. He has been on the faculty of Lynchburg College in Virginia since 2002 where he is a professor of accounting and the chairman of the accounting department. He enjoys outdoor activities with his wife and three sons, travel, photography, making music, and learning foreign languages (he speaks fluent technical Spanish).

Made in the USA
Columbia, SC
14 May 2020